CATHEDRALS
OF THE WORLD

One Hundred Historic Architectural Treasures

RAZIA GROVER

WORTH
PRESS

Contents

First published in 2010
by Worth Press Ltd

Concept, editorial, layout,
and design
© Worth Press Ltd 2010
www.worthpress.co.uk

This book was created by BookBuilder **3.**

Editor: Nirad Grover
Design: Malini Saigal
DTP: Arun Aggarwal

Every effort has been made to ensure the accuracy of the information presented in this book. The Publisher will not assume liability for damages caused by inaccuracies in the data and makes no warranty whatsoever expressed or implied. The Publisher welcomes comments and corrections from readers, emailed to info@worthpress.co.uk, which will be considered for incorporation in future editions. Likewise, every effort has been made to trace copyright holders and seek permission to use illustrative and other material. The Publisher wishes to apologize for any inadvertent errors or omissions and would be glad to rectify these in future editions.

Maps are for indicative purposes only and do not claim to represent authentic international boundaries.

Floorplans throughout - Copyright reserved for each individual castle.

British Library Cataloging in Publication Data: a catalog record for this book is available from the British Library

ISBN: 978-1-903025-98-7

Printed and bound in Singapore by Imago

CATHEDRALS – GATEWAYS TO HEAVEN

The Great Cathedrals of the world strive to capture in their awe-inspiring beauty the divine power of God and offer the promise of a glimpse of the splendours of Heaven. To the believers they are the divine houses of God for worship and prayer, to the visitors, architectural wonders of human creativity, craftsmanship and determination to achieve, almost, the impossible.

Late Gothic Pendant fan vault in Henry VII's chapel, (1503–19) with the stone fans as complete cones, hanging down like pendants. The chapel has been described as 'the most beautiful in all Christendom'. Westminster Abbey (11th c.) London, England.

Lancet – a slender more sharply pointed Gothic arch, always without tracery.

Less pointed Gothic arch, on cluster piers.

Ogee arch is formed by two S-shaped curves, one of which is flipped to meet the other at the highest point.

STAINED GLASS
Favoured by the church in the West, stained glass was used extensively since the 12th century and was considered to be a precious object and disserving a prominent place in the building.

RIGHT: Rose window filled with radiating tracery and stained glass pattern. Chartres Cathedral, France

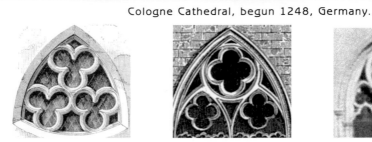

Crockets

Open Work Spires

Trancept Spire

Cologne Cathedral, begun 1248, Germany.

Trefoils

Quatrefoils

Cinquefoil over two trefoils

RIGHT: Ridge-rib vault, a decorative rib outlining the ridge of the vault, in the lofty interior of the cathedral at Rheims facing west towards the rose windows and dates from 1255–99,

Trancept roof

Apse or Chevet

Pinnacle

Flying Buttresses

Compound or Clustered Piers from Salisbury Cathedral, UK.

FOILS
Name given to each of the arcs used in Gothic tracery. The number of foils grouped together give the term *trefoil* (three arcs or lobes), *quatrefoil* (four), *cinquefoil* (five), and so on.

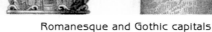

Romanesque and Gothic capitals

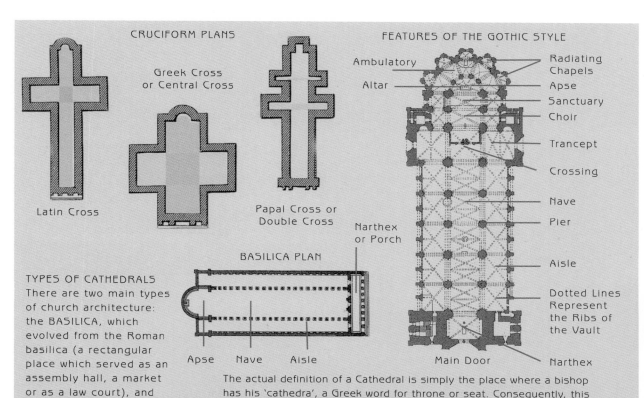

CRUCIFORM PLANS

Greek Cross or Central Cross

Latin Cross

Papal Cross or Double Cross

FEATURES OF THE GOTHIC STYLE

- Ambulatory
- Altar
- Radiating Chapels
- Apse
- Sanctuary
- Choir
- Trancept
- Crossing
- Nave
- Pier
- Narthex or Porch
- Aisle
- Dotted Lines Represent the Ribs of the Vault
- Main Door
- Narthex

BASILICA PLAN

Apse — Nave — Aisle

TYPES OF CATHEDRALS
There are two main types of church architecture: the BASILICA, which evolved from the Roman basilica (a rectangular place which served as an assembly hall, a market or as a law court), and the CRUCIFORM which is in the shape of a cross.

The actual definition of a Cathedral is simply the place where a bishop has his 'cathedra', a Greek word for throne or seat. Consequently, this place becomes a symbol of his authority. The size, the architectural style or location of a church is of no consequence in the selection process.

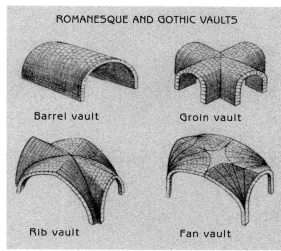

ROMANESQUE AND GOTHIC VAULTS

Barrel vault — Groin vault

Rib vault — Fan vault

Romanesque arches – Zigzag decoration from Durham Cathedral.

Byzantine and Romanesque elements merge to create these twisted, fluted and geometrically patterned columns.

Campanile, bell tower, free-standing and leaning during and ever since its constsruction

Pisa Cathedral, begun 1063, Italy. Stylistically, this refind group of buildings at Pisa are somewhat of an oddity in comparison to the sturdy Romanesque style. The white marble exterior is decorated with superimposed arcades of delicate columns and pilasters reminiscent of a more oriental style.

Round arches with simple geometric patterns on sturdy circular columns are characteristic of the Romanesque style.

ROMANESQUE & NORMAN 11th & 12th

The Romanesque style was prevalent in Europe in the 11th and 12th centuries. As the name suggests, Romanesque architecture grew out of the classical tradition of ancient Rome and its various revivals in subsequent centuries. Themes such as the semicircular arch, the apse and the tunnel vault were developed. Simple or richly decorated motifs from nature were represented in stone on different styles of capitals. In England, Romanesque architecture arrived with the Normans and is known as 'Norman'. The Norman Conquest of England, in 1066, by William the Conqueror, was followed by an intense religious building fervour. Durham Cathedral, begun 1093, although characteristically pure Norman, it is the first church to have ribbed vaulting throughout – a key feature in the transition to the Gothic style.

GOTHIC 12th to mid-16th c.

In Medieval times absolute faith was paramount. Whole communities and all trades, crafts and arts, are drawn into a single enterprise – the building of a cathedral in which to house and worship with proper ritual the relics of the local saint. The earthly architectural skills involved in the act of creating a Gothic Cathedral, was as much an allegory of the act of God being the supreme master-mason of all things. The symbolic 'light of the world' that radiated within the cathedral was made possible with the introduction of elegant flying buttresses which could support ribbed vaults over wide aisles and nave on a thin wall framework of great height, admitting light through large pointed or rose windows filled with stained glass and framed by delicate stone tracery. Pointed arches, spires, pinnacles, towers and statuary, are also essential elements of Gothic architecture.

CATHEDRALS—
ARCHITECTURAL ELEMENTS & STYLES

St. Mark's, 1063-1095. Venice. Originally a Basilica, was transformed into a cruciform plan by the addition of transepts. The splendour of Byzantine, Romanesque and Gothic architecture come together to create one of the most highly ornate and beautiful churches in Italy.

BYZANTINE
4th to 15th c.

Christianity was officially recognized by the Roman Emperor Constantine I, in 313, and in 326 it had become the official religion of the Roman Empire. The Emperor in 330 moved his capital to the Greek colony of Byzantium, at the eastern edge of Europe and renamed it Constantinople. The emerging religion adopted as its new place of worship the Roman Basilica – a rectangular assembly hall, at the east end of which a hemispherical apse became the Christian sanctuary. This was the forerunner of the cruciform plan which was established in early 10th century. Central domes and semi-domes became common features. The interiors were covered with decorations of immense richness – marble, mosaics, icons, frescoes and gold-leaf. Constantinople was captured by the Ottoman Turks in 1453 and was renamed Istanbul. The Byzantine architectural legacy is so embedded in the Eastern Christian Church, that it is still the prefered church building style of today.

TOP LEFT: St. Mark's Byzantine interior is adorned with coloured glass mosaics and gold-leaf backgrounds.

TOP RIGHT: Mosaic of the Emperor Justinian from the 6th century Byzantine Basilica of San Vitale, in Ravenna, Italy.

RIGHT: Ivan the Terrible's St. Basil's, in Moscow, was built with Byzantine architecture in mind and with Russian flavour in its realization with an impressive array of onion domes of many colours and patterns.

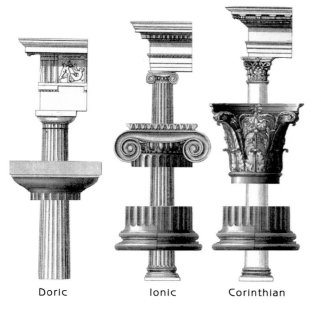

Doric Ionic Corinthian

THE THREE GREEK ORDERS
The architectural orders originated in ancient Greece, were widely used by the Romans, and remained the basic architectural style in the West until the end of the 19th century.
The main three Orders are the Doric, the Ionic and the Corinthian.
A simplified version of the Doric was widely used by the Etruscans and it is called the Tuscan. While a combined Corinthian capital with Ionic spiral scrolls at its top is known as Composite

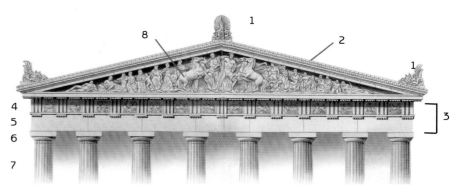

CLASSICAL TEMPLE PEDIMENT
Pediment is a triangular low-pitched gable, mainly placed at the end of a roof or above a portico. Since the Renaissance smaller decorative pediments appeared above doors and windows.

1. Acroterion
2. Cornice
3. Entablature
4. Frieze
5. Architrave
6. Capital
7. Column
8. Tympanum

DOMES
1. Bruneleski's Early Renaissance dome of Santa Maria del Fiore, 1420–1436. Florence.
2. Michelangelo's Late Renaissance Dome of St. Peter's, 1547–1589. Rome.

Broken Pediment, a feature of the Baroque style.

GREEK AND ROMAN DECORATIVE MOTIFS
1. Meander
2. Egg-and-dart
3. Palmettes and lotus flowers
4. Cyma recta with Roman ornament and fusarole

Pediment over portico — Lantern
Dome

Bell tower
Clock tower

Pediment over window

Paired Corinthian Pilasters

Paired Corinthian Columns

Sir Christopher Wren's Baroque Cathedral of St. Paul's, 1675–1710. London.

RENAISSANCE & BAROQUE
15th to 17th c.

RENAISSANCE is the term that means the rebirth of the classical ideals and a return to harmony and balance. That came about by the rediscovery of Greek and Roman texts and research into newly excavated classical statuary and architecture. This interest originated in Italy and soon spread to many European countries. The architectural elements of the Greco-Roman world were revived and improvised upon – the classical orders (Doric, Ionic, Corinthian and Composite), the decorative motifs, the round arches and the barrel vaults. The pointed pediment gained new variations – the semi-circular cornice at its top, and, the Baroque style gave it the many-faceted broken pediment effect. In church architecture the Latin Cross and the Greek Cross retained their popularity.

BAROQUE originated in Rome in the 17th century and soon spread to other continents. The intellectual formulas offered by the Renaissance were put aside for a new dynamic architectural experience that appealed not only to the intellect but also to the emotions, with the creation of spacial illusions, symbolic schemes, repetition and distortion of classical motifs.

NEO-CLASSICAL
18th to 19th c.

The NEO-CLASSICAL style reacted against the excesses of Baroque and Rococo (a much more ornate offspring of Baroque). It was based on intellectual enquiry – the thorough study of ancient buildings and aimed for structural purity and simplicity by the removal or minimal use of ornamentation. Neo-classicism in America (1780–1860) provided the perfect expression for state and federal buildings. Most notable is the Capitol building in Washington (1792–1817).

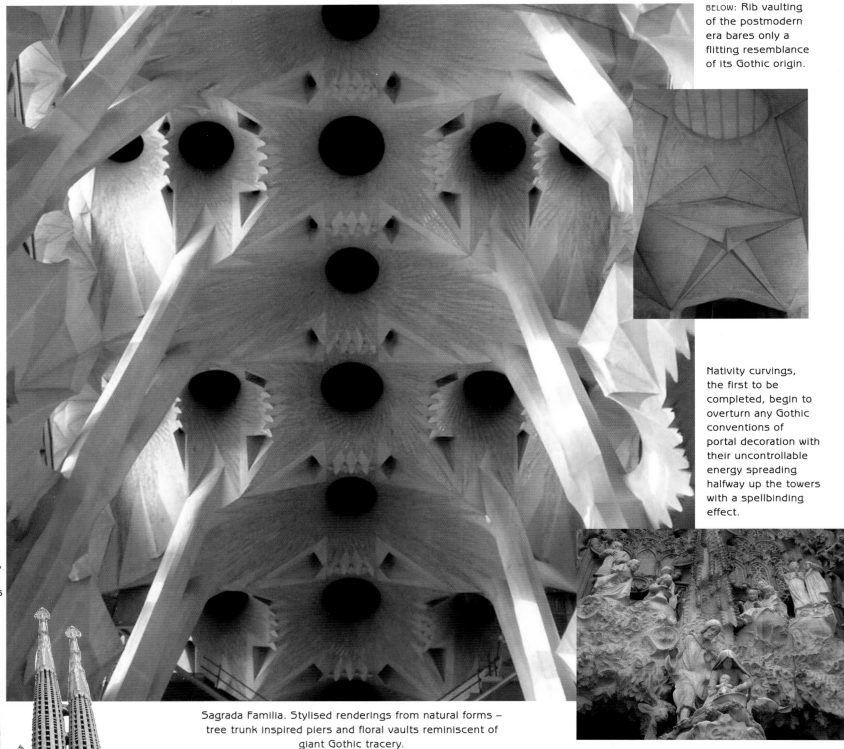

Nativity curvings, the first to be completed, begin to overturn any Gothic conventions of portal decoration with their uncontrollable energy spreading halfway up the towers with a spellbinding effect.

BELOW: Tilted columns acting as flying buttresses give support to the four towers above the Passion sculptures and create at the same time a protective portico. Sagrada Familia is due for completion in 2026, to celebrate the centenary of Gaudi's death.

Sagrada Familia. Stylised renderings from natural forms – tree trunk inspired piers and floral vaults reminiscent of giant Gothic tracery.

Sagrada Familia in Barcelona, Spain. Antoni Gaudi, in 1882 was commissioned to complete the Sagrada Familia. He overturned the original Neo-Gothic plans of the previous architects and re-invented the cathedral with a vision that embraced modern design solutions – reinterpretation of the Gothic piers, vaults and spires by the use of new stylised forms from nature. Gaudi created a unique and awesome vision belonging to the realms of creative fantasy and imagination that elevates the human spirit.

NEO–GOTHIC
18th to 21st c.

The revival of the Gothic style came gradually during the second half of the 18th century. Its emergence as the dominant alternative force to the Neoclassical tradition, allowed it once again, in the 19th century, to become the prefered style of Church building in many parts of the world. The interest in all aspects of the Middle Ages, is partly attributed to the writings and cultural activities of the architect Viollet-le-Duc (1814-1879). His reference work on the principles of Gothic art and architecture, exerted an informed influence on the next generation of architects, including Antoni Gaudi (1852–1926), who re-defined the Neo-Gothic style with his visionary work on the Cathedral of the Sagrada Familia in Barcelona, Spain. Viollet-le-Duc was commissioned to restore in 1844, among other churches and cathedrals, the Notre Dame of Paris. The gargoyles at the top of the towers are his invention.

11

Cordoba. The dome over the bay in front of the niche of the prayer hall. A skeleton of four pairs of curved and interlocking ribs, structurally necessitates the creation of a second smaller dome to fill the space in between. Intricate arabesque decorations and holy inscriptions cover the entire dome.

LEFT: Cordoba, the Great Mosque. Spain. Simple arches on ground level and interlocking multi-lobed (multi-foiled) arches above, form part of the arcade through which the niche of the prayer hall can be seen, indicating the direction of Mecca and is the focus of the whole building.

Crystal Cathedral, 1977–1980, California, USA. The Spire was built in 1990. Ultra modern in its concept and use of materials, echoes in a way the lofty heights of pointed Gothic towers.

ISLAM & MOORISH Spain 8th to 15th c.

Within a century after its foundation in AD 622 the Islamic world stretched from the frontiers of Central Asia and India to the Atlantic coast of southern Spain. With stylistic influences from the cultures it came in contact with, Islam developed a new distinctive culture of its own. Religious principles prohibit anthropomorphic representations and other living beings except plants. Plants together with abstract symbolic geometric patterns and Arabic inscriptions are a few of the striking features found in Islamic architecture. Other characteristic elements are the arches – horseshoe shaped, refered to as Moorish, multi-foiled and intertwined. The Great Mosque in Cordoba founded in the 8th c. and added to over the next two centuries, is an architectural masterpiece which set the standard for all other sacred buildings in Moorish Spain. Islamic rule in Spain continued until 1492.

CONTEBPORARY 20th to 21st c.

The temple, the cathedral and the mosque in previous centuries and cultures were statements of pride and defined a nation's identity. Creative ingenuity in our time is concentrated mostly on secular symbols of pride and power – the commercial skyscraper. Among the few noteworthy examples of religious building in the modern style, is the Crystal Cathedral, in California. Minimalist in decorative terms, clad in nothing but reflective glass, this dynamic structure evokes an intense sense of weightlessness in its ability to reflect the elements and blend into the landscape. The tower consists of stainless steel prisms, highly polished to capture and reflect light from all directions. A contemporary concept that should encourage other ecclesiastical architecture world-wide to look for inspiration in the architecture of their own times.

RIGHT: The Hammerbeam roof framework is definitely the most advanced form of late Gothic roof design.

RIGHT: The Baroque BALDACCHINO 1624–33, with its ogee-shaped canopy supported by four twisted columns, sits over the high altar and below Michelangelo's dome. Gianlorenzo Bernini, St Peter's, Rome.

This extraordinary octagonal lantern is supported by the monumental octagonal wooden vault of Ely Cathedral. This central space was added in 1322–1346, and has been called 'the only Gothic dome'.

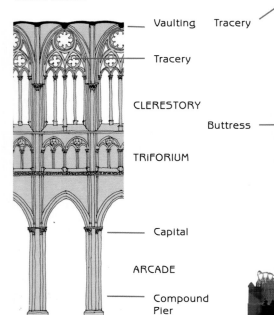

Vaulting

Tracery

Tracery

CLERESTORY

TRIFORIUM

Capital

ARCADE

Compound Pier

GOTHIC WALL ELEVATION

Bell tower

Lancet windows

Buttress

Gargoyles: Viollet-le-Duc's eerie gargoyles were added to Notre-Dame in the 1850s and 1860s.

Rose windows

Gallery of 28 statues of the Kings of Israel

Portals with deep set pointed arches carved with statues

GARGOYLES AND GROTESQUES
Gargoyle figures originally functioned as disguised gutterstones to traject rainwater away from the walls. Over the years evolved into the leering bestiary and grotesques we see today, depicting the horrors of afterlife and damnation.

A night view of Notre-Dame, 1163–1330. Paris.

GOTHIC WINDOWS
Gothic archtecture is defined by its ornate window tracery and vaulting.

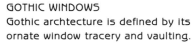

Gothic decorative motifs

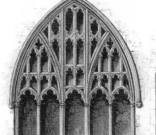
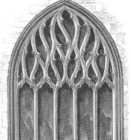

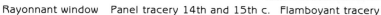

Lancet windows   13th and 14th century tracery supported by slender mullions (bars)   Rayonnant window   Panel tracery 14th and 15th c.   Flamboyant tracery

Introduction

"And I John saw the Holy City, the new Jerusalem coming down from God out of Heaven adorned as a bride for her husband." The words of St John the Apostle, recorded in the Book of Revelation are enshrined in the liturgy for the consecration of a church. Prophetic words for they conjure up an image of what the earliest of churches comprising the Christian followers of Jesus after his death and resurrection were to become. Not only in size and numbers, as the faith spread far and wide, but in its physical manifestation of the spiritual and artistic aspirations of man, the church was the embodiment of the Lord's spiritual kingdom, His bride. The great cathedrals of the world are the glorious culmination of this vision, from their earliest beginnings as mere shrines or makeshift houses of prayer. The golden era of cathedral building was the Middle Ages, that lasted for about five centuries from the 11th to the 16th century. Although England and Europe were the main theater of cathedral building, these masterpieces of Christian architecture have since been built right up to modern times in all parts of the world.

Cathedral of St Étienne, Sens, France.

THE CATHEDRAL

In the hierarchy of the Christian church, the cathedral is the seat (*cathedra*) of a bishop. It was the mother church of the diocese and the core of community life. It offered teaching and guidance, protection, and comfort. In its early days the nave could be used to transact business or confer degrees, while the crypt sheltered pilgrims, the sick, and even refugees. It was frequently the oldest building in the town, and certainly the most imposing, the towering landmark visible from all around. Today, as then, it usually serves as a meeting place for its governing body, the chapter—English cathedrals had their own Chapter House attached to or part of the cathedral complex. Baptisms took place here, coronations, and celebratory or funeral masses or services. Today, the church choir is often the finest in the city (or state) and much sought after in its cultural life. Both the church bells and the organ occupy pride of place among a cathedral's assets. The clergy of the cathedral itself was divided into the monastic and the secular orders. The first followed the rules and vows of the order and the clergy resided on the premises. The second was bound by a secular code of statutes or canons, as is the case today. Before the Reformation, all cathedrals of Western Europe belonged to the church of Rome governed by the Pope. In England, the dissolution of monasteries by Henry VIII gave birth to the Anglican Church of England. In Europe, the break with Catholicism was ushered in by Martin Luther and the Calvinists. The majority of cathedrals belong to either the Roman Catholic or Protestant (and its splinter groups) dispensation today.

ORIGIN OF THE CATHEDRAL FORM

The cathedral has its origins in the Roman basilica. Constantine, the first Christian Roman emperor established Rome as the center of the Eastern Roman Empire. Once Christianity was officially recognized, the followers of Christ, who had been forced to practice furtively till then, were now able to build large and handsome places of worship. The basilica emerged as a major form in ecclesiastical architecture. Its basic plan comprised a central nave, an aisle on either side, and an apse at the sanctuary end. The structure was surrounded by a forecourt. St Peter's, built (4th century) over the burial place of Peter the Apostle was among the earliest of such basilicas until it was replaced in the early 16th century by the edifice we see today. Not technically a cathedral (that honor goes to St John Lateran among Rome's churches), it is considered the holiest site in Christendom as it honors the apostle regarded as the first bishop and first Pope. The Basilica of San Vitale in Ravenna is another, later example.

PRE-ROMANESQUE PERIOD

As the church evolved with additions and modifications, so did the styles. Preceding the first of the major stylistic genres, the Romanesque, were the Early Christian, the Carolingian and the Ottonian. Carolingian refers to the cultural renaissance in north Europe in the 8th and 9th centuries inspired by Charlemagne and Louis the Pious. A conscious attempt was made to emulate past Roman and Byzantine styles. The Aachen basilica-cathedral, in plan and opulence, is the most notable example. Ottonian architecture, belonging to the reign of Emperor Otto the Great (936-75 CE) drew from the Carolingian and Byzantine examples and

THE CATHEDRAL MAKERS

Who were the people behind the great cathedrals? Very often there is no architect's name. It was a meeting of many minds and resources. The king, a nobleman, abbot, or bishop initiated the project. Many men of the church themselves were equally talented in scholarship and religious doctrine as in the technical possibilities of the day. The profession of the architect only emerged after the 13th century when identities of individuals were established. Until then and for a long while after it was the master mason who master-minded the design and construction. The 13th-century Villard de Honnecourt compiled an invaluable sketchbook of drawings for teaching masons. Cathedrals were the product of many generations and there were families of architects or craftsmen who carried on the project, such as the Parlers of Prague or the Roritzers of Regensburg. Money, when not given by a wealthy patron or the state, was collected through bequests or rents, or even taxes imposed on themselves by bishops. Notre-Dame in Paris is said to be built with widows' sous!

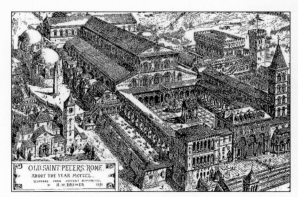

A 19th-century reconstruction of the 4th-century St Peter's Basilica.

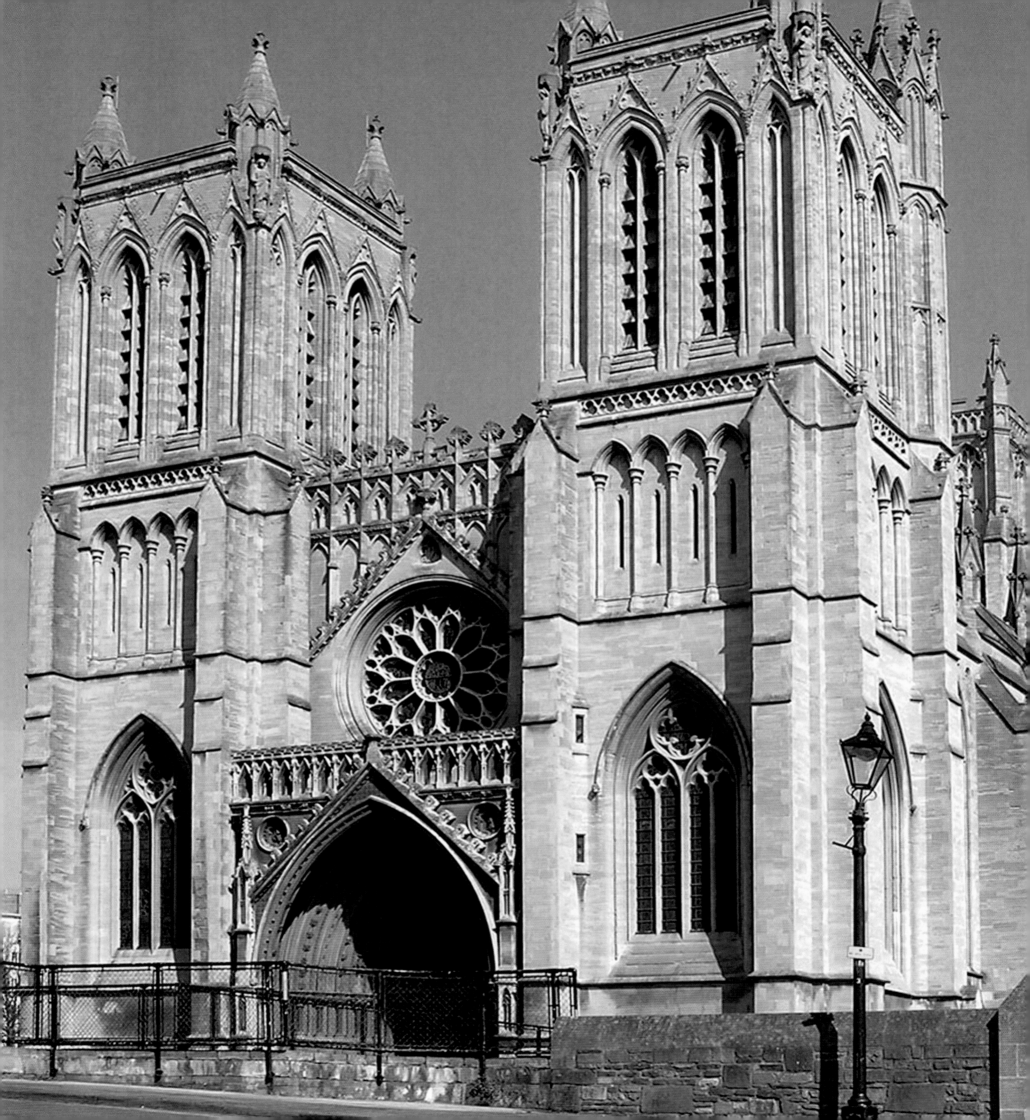

examples and lasted from the mid 10th to mid 11th century, particularly in Germany and Belgium. Both styles are part of the history of many of the cathedrals featured in this book. Charlemagne's dream of a unified empire was shattered by the Norman invasion. Mainland Europe splintered into independent kingdoms, each seeking to secure its own future by breaking with the past. Medieval towns sprung up on the strength of trade and feudal bounty. Prosperity, and the spread of Christianity fueled by the Crusades, resulted in the development of ecclesiastical architecture, and a new cohesive order — the Romanesque.

THE ANGLO-NORMAN CATHEDRAL

England in the meantime was just embarking on one of the most exciting periods in her architectural history, personified by the cathedral, the chief of all art forms. Because of her isolated position from mainland Europe there was a unified tradition, within which the architecture evolved (relevant too for Scotland, Wales, and Ireland). Monasteries and abbey churches were widespread before the Norman Conquest (1066 CE). Following William the Conqueror's victory at the battle of Hastings, there was an intense period of building activity when older churches were repaired or extended, and new ones built. Now, as later, erstwhile wooden churches were being regularly destroyed by fire because of their predominant use of wood. The general basilican plan was enlarged eastward at the sanctuary end either with apses (Canterbury, Lincoln, Ely) or ambulatories with radiating chapels (Winchester, Gloucester), with changes in the interior too. Norman cathedrals gave the impression of heaviness because of their thick walls and towers but there was nevertheless a homely, human quality about them due to the relative low height and compact interior. The English were, however, preoccupied with linearity and as time went on this was expressed through lengthening the nave and inventing the Perpendicular style. To the English also goes the honor of inventing the ribbed vault (Durham), an improvement on the old wooden framework over the central nave; vaulting later became the common method of roofing other areas too. Another original English feature was the lantern tower placed at the crossing of the transept, also at Durham, and other churches.

EXPERIMENTING WITH THE ROMANESQUE

The Romanesque period, overlapping with the development of English cathedrals, ushered in experimentation both on the isle and on mainland Europe. A basic parameter thus far had been the use of the cathedral for ceremonial purposes. Religious ceremonial was now reduced, eliminating the need for a second transept at the western end. The trend now was in favor of larger, individual buildings in place of the several places of worship associated with the widespread cult of relics. The eastern end was extended through ambulatories and chapels. Thick walls were lightened by a multiplicity of windows as well as openings on more levels. Naves, aisles, and bays increased, necessitating stone vaulting and arcades for extra support. The western front was established as the principal entry point with emphasis given to the portal (with one or more entry doors). The bell tower, initially surmounting only the entrance façade, was now replicated by towers at other points such as the crossing or ends of transepts (albeit without bells). These developed their own contours as they soared upwards, to be capped with spires, the prominent harbinger of the cathedral. As technique and tools evolved, so did the aspirations of clients and patrons. The element of verticality translated religious passion, generous funding, and competence into an aesthetic, and Gothic was born.

THE GOTHIC

Attaining ever increasing heights and emphasizing movement, Gothic architecture became synonymous with cathedrals of the 12th to 16th centuries. No other style was so expressive of the spiritual and transcendental ethos of religious architecture. It represented the cultural and intellectual flowering of an emerging urbanism from the 12th century onwards. Except for Italy, where the influence of classic Rome prevailed, and Spain, which was subject to a variety of influences — Moorish, French, German — the pure Gothic spirit fired the imagination of abbots and bishops, rulers and patrons, architects and master masons, and the people themselves. The very first Gothic expression of significance is the choir of St Denis in France conceived by Abbot Suger in 1144. Gothic was dynamic, inventive, and affected not only the architecture but all the arts — stained-glass windows, sculpture, and church furniture. Complex vaulting systems, the flying buttress, the pointed arch, resolved

Stained-glass window at the basilica of St Denis, Paris, depicting Abbot Suger.

Facing page:
Bristol Cathedral, Bristol, England.

structural and also stylistic issues, while stained glass (and later gray glass) was a means of manipulating light; it was also an instructive medium through its imagery for the illiterate. The rose window was now introduced at the ends of transepts, also allowing light to filter in, thus merging these side volumes with the main. Externally, repetitive architectural and decorative elements in an ascending order defied the laws of gravity as they rose from earth to sky, culminating in the spires, which themselves were works of art. The movement was led by France (eg, Chartres, Bourges, Reims, Laon); Germany (eg, Cologne, Mainz, Speyer, Worms) followed suit, though Romanesque forms lingered on. Others (Austria, Hungary, Poland, Scandinavia, Netherlands, Belgium) too, were influenced by France.

POST GOTHIC AND REGIONAL VARIATIONS

Elements of Renaissance art had already crept in before the fading away of Gothic in the 16th century. Italy never really adopted the Gothic style. The monastic orders — Dominicans, Franciscans — largely presided over cathedral building here. The basic plan of the basilica was followed. Also, the sunny Mediterranean climate did not require the opening up of interior spaces to permit light as in the Gothic style. A greater degree of horizontal massing was the norm. St Peter's and Florence Cathedral exemplify the heritage of classical antiquity and Renaissance imagery to which Italian cathedrals belong. Spain borrowed greatly from French models (Bourges→Toledo; Reims→León). The Moorish influence also predominated, particularly in southern Spain; mosques were known to provide the footprint for cathedrals built on the same site, while elements of Islamic decoration were imaginatively retained. Regional schools of craftsmanship, such as the *mujédar* and Plateresque, left their imprint. Spanish cathedrals also impress with their size as they were part of complexes that included the cloister, the cemetery, and innumerable subsidiary buildings; the bell tower, too, having supplanted the Muslim minaret in some cases, was an independent structure. Among them, Seville is considered the largest cathedral in the world (founded early 15th century).

THE MODERN AGE

Cathedrals exist in most countries today. Some cities could have two, affiliated either to the Protestant or Roman Catholic denomination, as in Melbourne and Sydney. The Eastern Orthodox Church, with its own variant of the Christian doctrine, is represented by a unique architectural expression of the cathedral — the multiple domes — as well as the decoration, rich with icons of Byzantine influence. The revival of older styles clothed in contemporary idioms expresses itself in variations such as the Neo-Gothic or Neo-Classic. Modern architecture of the 19th and 20th centuries has cast its own stamp on cathedrals, such as the Rock Cathedral of Helsinki, and the mega cathedrals of America and South America. Nothing, however, quite compares with the great cathedrals of the Medieval Age though each has a fascinating story to tell. These splendid legacies of history, art, architecture, and society are still best summed up the words of John Harvey written 60 years ago: "A cathedral was not a church alone; it was the greatest of art galleries, the noblest of lecture halls, sublimest of opera houses. The best of sculpture, of painting, of music and of verse were not too good for its service. Its enrichment provoked the finest flights of the decorative artists. It was in the cathedral, above all buildings, that architecture was truly the mistress art."

THE CATHEDRAL AS MUSEUM

Few of the great and interesting cathedrals are sparse in their decorative aspects. The great collections of art, sculpture, and religious artifacts that weave into the tapestry of the buildings merit the attention of museologists. And indeed some do form part of the national galleries of the countries where they belong. Wars and other man-made or natural disasters have taken their toll, so that much is now either stored in the crypt or treasury and not freely accessible. Restoration efforts have done much to preserve and restore the architecture, while precious originals have been replicated for common view, both on the exterior (as the four horses on Milan Cathedral) or inside. Nevertheless, an extraordinary wealth of sculpture, paintings and frescoes, mosaics, woodwork and ironwork, glasswork, fragments purporting to be pieces of the True Cross or garments of saints, reliquaries containing the hand or finger of saintly figures, all still enrich these great monuments to Christianity. Today, as before, the cathedral, old or new, is a fascinating record of historical fact, legend, artistic style, decorative craftsmanship, and community spirit. Above all, however, cathedrals are the enduring symbols of the power of the church down the ages.

Notre-Dame Cathedral, Paris.

Mudéjar architecture in Cathedral of the Savior, Zaragoza, Spain.

REPAIR AND RESTORATION

Most of the great medieval cathedrals were built part by part, sometimes over a period of centuries. During this time, frequent modifications and repairs were also carried out. The restoration of medieval buildings as an art began as a movement in France in the early 19th century. Viollet-le-Duc was much sought after for the restoration of several cathedrals and other buildings. Paris's Notre'Dame brought him national recognition. He believed in recreating layers of history that may not have actually existed but logically should have been built. His theory was strongly debated by proponents of the John Ruskin school who argued that the past can never be faithfully recreated. Following the massive destruction of cathedrals in the two World Wars restoration became a major industry and remains an ongoing activity.

Facing page:
Cathedral of St Sebastian, Rio de Janeiro, Brazil.

Tympanum, Toledo Cathedral, Spain.

Rood-screen, Church of St Étienne-du-Mont, Paris, France.

Pulpit, St John the Baptist Cathedral, Yaroslavl, Russia.
Facing page: Interior of Albi Cathedral, France.

The reredos in the sanctuary of St Francis Cathedral, Santa Fe, New Mexico.

Retable of St Margaret, St Léonce Cathedral, Fréjus, France.

AUSTRALIA

Canberra

Melbourne

St Patrick's Cathedral

Twelve years after the city of Melbourne was founded, its diocese was created as a suffragan see to the Archdiocese of Sydney. The Augustinian Father James Goold was consecrated as the first bishop in the existing St Francis' Church, which was accorded the status of a cathedral. This soon proved to be too small for the population, which was primarily Roman Catholic. The gold rush and independence of Victoria from New South Wales provided the desired funds and impetus for a larger building and with land granted for a new church and school on the same site, Father Goold's vision for a new building began to see the light of day. Plans were prepared by one firm of architects after another until the arrival of William Wardell, a devout Catholic himself and specialist in ecclesiastical architecture. His design for a grand cathedral was to be realized in two stages. He, however, did not live to see its completion; this task was accomplished by Archbishop Carr and his successors.

Wardell saw St Patrick's as a magnificent building, larger in scale than its counterparts in England or Ireland. The plan is traditionally cruciform, and there are two apparent styles—the plainer Early English Gothic, financially more viable, and the later Geometric Decorated. The nave and aisles came first, followed by the rest. The original west door was a double doorway, according to Wardell symbolic of both the human and divine nature of Christ. This was later changed to a single opening. Ceremonies were held to mark the completion of the main sections.

NAME	St Patrick's Cathedral
ADDRESS	Cnr Gisborne St & Cathedral Place, East Melbourne VIC 3002, Australia
CONSTRUCTION HISTORY	**1858** Cathedral begun
	1868 Nave complete; double entrance doorway changed to single
	1897 Consecrated
	1917–39 Interior completed; spires built; cathedral complete
ARCHITECT	William Wilkinson Wardell
MATERIALS	Local stone
STYLE	Gothic Revival

In later years, reforms in liturgical practises influenced alterations in the interior, allowing for extended spaces. In 1974 the Pope conferred the title of a minor basilica on the cathedral, which was blessed with a visit from Pope John Paul II in 1986. Upgrading and restoration works were completed by 1997.

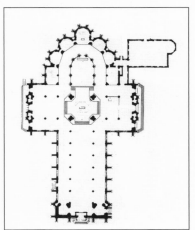

Facing page:
St Patrick's Gothic towers soar upwards uncluttered by undue embellishments.

Statue of St Francis of Assisi on the grounds of the cathedral.

The massive organ above the entrance doorway.

AUSTRALIA

Sydney

Canberra

St Mary's Cathedral

Sydney was colonized by the British in 1788 as a penal settlement and its spiritual needs initially administered by a chaplain from the Church of England. Many of its settlers and convicts however were Roman Catholic but it was only in 1820 that an Irish Catholic pastor arrived. He is said to have had a vision of a grand church in golden stone dedicated to the Virgin Mary to be built in the city, so he applied for land, which was granted to him. The foundation stone of the first Gothic-style church was laid in 1821. Under the first archbishop, John Polding, the church was modified 30 years later by the acclaimed Gothic Revivalist, Augustus Welby Pugin, but less than two decades later it was destroyed by fire. It was at this stage that the architect William Wardell, a disciple of Pugin's, was commissioned to prepare a new design.

St Mary's is a unique example of a change in orientation in the plan of the church. Though conventionally cruciform, the traditional west front lies to the south and the choir to the north. Twin towers surmount the main entrance, where there are three portals. Additional entry points lie at each end of the transepts. The cathedral's architecture borrows from both English and French models. Public entry is usually from the Hyde Park entrance at the west, where Gothic windows with pointed arches and richly decorated doors lead the eye upwards to flying buttresses and a pitched slate roof. Inside, the timber ceiling offsets the stonework; heads of saints meet at the apex of arches; four chapels are ornately carved; and the mosaic flooring is exceptionally striking.

Statues, a painting of Jesus Christ, and stained-glass windows adorn the sanctuary.

NAME	St Mary's Cathedral
ADDRESS	College St, Sydney, Australia
CONSTRUCTION HISTORY	**1821–68** 1st 1st Gothic church begun; design modified; burnt down; temporary wooden church built; burnt down
	1868–2000 Present cathedral built; consecrated 1882; spires completed 2000
COMMISSIONED BY	Archbishop Polding
ARCHITECT	William Wilkinson Wardell
MATERIALS	Local sandstone; red cedar roof; ceiling vault in timber; Moruya granite small columns
STYLE	Gothic Revival, Geometric Decorated

Many of the beautiful details and treasures of the cathedral were added in the 20th century, including several stained-glass windows. The nave was finally completed in 1928 and two years later, Pope Pius XI bestowed on the cathedral the title of a minor basilica. In 2000, the spires were finally completed.

Facing page:
St Mary's stands on the site of the first Roman Catholic chapel in Australia.

One of the 14 paintings depicting the stages of Jesus's crucifixion.

AUSTRIA

Vienna

Gurk

Gurk Cathedral

The small town of Gurk nestles among the green valleys of southern Austria, where the saintly Hemma was born in the court of Emperor St Henry II. Tragic events in her life—the sudden death of her husband and later that of her son in battle—moved her to donate her wealth and pursue a spiritual life. Among her religious acts she built a convent where she lived till the end of her life (1045), and a small church dedicated to the Virgin Mary, where she lies buried. Her tomb soon became a place of pilgrimage and she was beatified by the church in 1287 as miracles increasingly began to be attributed to her. Almost 100 years later the church was given the status of a cathedral, and in time various architectural and interior elements added to it.

This little gem of Romanesque architecture with details in Gothic and Baroque has a straightforward exterior, distinguished by its twin west towers and their onion domes. The barrel-vaulted porch was enclosed in 1348, and later painted inside. A magnificent collection of murals dating to later periods decorate interior surfaces of the church and depict episodes from the Old and New Testaments. The story of Hemma is painted on wooden reliefs. Most spectacular of all is the High Altar with 72 statues and 82 faces of angels, and which, during Holy Week, is covered with a veil painted with 99 biblical scenes.

NAME	Gurk Cathedral & Shrine of St Hemma
ADDRESS	Domkustodie Salvatorianerkolleg, Dompaltz 11, 9342 Gurk, Austria
CONSTRUCTION HISTORY	1140–1200 Cathedral built
	1626–38 High Altar made
	1682 Onion domes built
	1740 Pulpit and altar at end of nave added
COMMISSIONED BY	Original church: Hemma
MATERIALS	Stone
STYLE	Romanesque, Gothic, Baroque

Saint Hemma's beautifully decorated sarcophagus was placed under the altar in the crypt of the cathedral in *c.* 1720. Along with the Episcopal Chapel in the south tower it can only be seen on guided tours. St Hemma was finally canonized in 1938. Her feast day falls on 27 June but Gurk Cathedral celebrates it two days later on 29 June! The church was blessed by a visit of the Pope in 1988, when he conducted a mass here for 80,000 pilgrims.

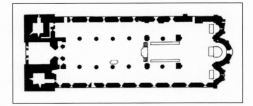

Facing page:
Dedicated to the Virgin Mary, Gurk Cathedral nestles in the valleys of southern Austria and shelters the shrine of a beloved Austrian saint.

One of the two symmetrical towers of the cathedral , this one has an inbuilt clock.

A drawing of the sumptuous main altar in the cathedral.

AUSTRIA

Vienna

St Stephen's

St Stephen's Cathedral

The elevation of St Stephen's from a parish church to the status of a cathedral was for many years denied to the people of Vienna by the bishops of Passau. It was not until 1469 that the Diocese of Vienna was created, with St Stephen's as its mother church. The cathedral stands on the ruins of two earlier churches, the first of the 12th century, which was built on the site of a Romanesque sanctuary. The second structure expanded the earlier building westwards in the mid 13th century, but when burnt was replaced by a larger church, using some of the older Romanesque elements. The choir, vaulting of the nave, and the south tower were added later. Work stopped on the north tower in 1511, which is why the church looks strangely imbalanced.

Giant's Door is the main entrance to the church. Owing to the mix of original and reconstructed parts, the church's architecture ranges from Romanesque to Gothic. Inside, Anton Pilgram's stone pulpit is outstanding as is the 1447 Wiener Neustadter wooden altarpiece among a total of 18 altars. The strange 17th-century tomb of Emperor Frederick III sculpted with hideous goblins, a Byzantine icon of Mary and Jesus, and a figure of Christ with an agonized expression, known as *Christ with a Toothache*, are all striking highlights. A most remarkable feature is the diamond patterned tiled roof, so steeply sloped that snow seldom collects on it. The crypt and catacombs bear the remains of over 11,000 persons who died in the plague of 1735.

NAME	St Stephen's Cathedral (Stephansdom)
ADDRESS	Stephansplatz, 1st District, Vienna, Austria
CONSTRUCTION HISTORY	**1144–47** 1st church built and consecrated
	13th century Westward extension; fire
	14th century Choir consecrated 1340; **extended** westwards; south tower begun
	15th century South tower (Alter Steffl or Old Steve) completed; nave vaulted
	1579 North tower unfinished but crowned
COMMISSIONED BY	Duke Rudolph IV
MATERIALS	Limestone, stone pulpit, wooden altar, steel frame tiled roof
STYLE	Romanesque, Gothic, Baroque interior

Mozart was married here in 1782 and his funeral service also held nine years later. His association with the cathedral is listed in detail on a memorial tablet. The building escaped planned demolition at the hands of the retreating German army at the end of World War II though the slender south tower spire was shelled. Fire from nearby plundered shops spread to the roof and choir but harmed few of its artistic treasures. The church was reopened in 1952 after restoration.

Mosaic of the double-headed eagle symbolic of the empire ruled from Vienna by the Habsburg dynasty.

The pulpit, with sculptures of the saints Gregory, Jerome, and Augustine.

Facing page:
Its roof gloriously covered with mosaic tiles, St Stephen's Cathedral is Vienna's most important religious building.

Salzburg Cathedral

Salzburg Cathedral evokes many events from Mozart's life—it was here that he was baptized, served briefly as its organist, and performed several of his works for the first time, including the *Coronation Mass*. The building's ancestry however goes back ten centuries to a large church of 774 CE built under St Virgil. Eight times over the course of about 800 years it was severely damaged either by lightning or fire and its ultimate destruction in 1598 gave rise to an ambitious scheme for a building that would accommodate the entire population of Salzburg. This was modified and built in stages under successive archbishops. Finally, the present building was completed by an Italian architect and opened by Prince Archbishop Paris Lodron in 1628, with the towers appearing a few years later.

When Virgil Dom, the first Romanesque ancestor of the cathedral was built in the 8th century it was already considered large, and its successors attempted to retain that status. The church is divided into three units, each with its own gate. The towers, too, have three units each, bearing clocks and bells. Paintings, stucco work, statues, and frescoes add to its glory both within and on the exterior. There are four chapels on either side. The highlight is the green dome, which, along with the towers, make the cathedral a commanding symbol of Salzburg against the backdrop of the range of hills beyond.

NAME	Salzburg Cathedral
ADDRESS	Residenzplatz, Salzburg, Austria
CONSTRUCTION HISTORY	**767–74 CE** 1st church (Virgil Dom)
	785–821 CE Renovated; struck by lightning (842 CE)
	1000–1020 Extended
	12th century Towers added; burnt and rebuilt
	1598 Completely burnt
	1611–1628 Present cathedral built and consecrated
COMMISSIONED BY	Archbishop Markus Sittikus Count Hohenems
ARCHITECT	Santino Solari
MATERIALS	Stone, Untersberg marble-like stone façade
STYLE	Renaissance, Baroque

Damaged again by fire in 1859 and bombed during World War II, causing the dome to collapse, the cathedral was restored to its original design after the war. Its prized possession is the old organ of 1703, though the one now in use was made in 1988. The Domplatz (cathedral square), a masterpiece of urban design, is mous for the staging of the play *Jedermann* (Everyman) during the annual Salzburg Festival, and for the popular Christmas Market.

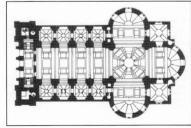

Facing page:
Dedicated to St Rupert of Salzburg, the cathedral, designed by an Italian architect, is built in a modern Italian Baroque idiom.

Baroque in ornamentation, each wall painting is framed within its own architectural space.

Stone carving and Baroque frescoes merge seamlessly together in a work of Renaissance perfection.

Tournai

Brussels

BELGIUM

Office du Tourisme

Caisse d'Epargne de la Ville de Tournai

Tournai Cathedral

Showpiece of two of the most important architectural styles of medieval Europe, Tournai Cathedral in Normandy is last in the line of many places of worship that have stood on its site before. A pagan temple is believed to have preceded the first church built in the 8th century, which was followed by another a century later. Destruction by fire brought about the rebuilding of successive houses of worship. During a major plague in the 11th century the church was used as a place of refuge. The Romanesque model only came about in the 12th century, when the church became a cathedral. The dedication to Our Lady was made following the plague when the bishop led a great procession through the cathedral in gratitude to her as several miraculous cures had been effected in her name. The procession is still held annually.

The cathedral's architecture spans three separate styles in a pleasingly compatible manner—Romanesque, Early English Gothic (because Normandy was under English rule), and French Gothic. The French influence is most evident in the new choir, which extended the original Romanesque building. Borrowing the ground plan from the Soissons cathedral, which had only a small area for the choir, the architect arranged the radiating chapels around the ambulatory under one vault to save space, yet giving the impression of expansiveness. The straight chapels were located between the buttresses. Unfortunately, due to shortage of finances, the nave could not also be remodeled. Paintings by Rubens, medieval tapestries, and a Byzantine cross adorn the interior, but the highlight of the church is the Shrine of Our Lady, its covering beautifully sculpted in gold.

The western porch is surmounted by a rose window sculpted in the stone wall.

NAME	Cathedral of Our Lady (Cathédrale Notre-Dame)
ADDRESS	Place de l'Evêché 1, 7500 Tournai, Belgium
CONSTRUCTION HISTORY	**761 CE** 1st church on site
	1141–1198 Romanesque cathedral built; consecrated 1198
	13th century Stained-glass windows, Gothic choir added
	14th century Western porch transepts
	1777 Nave completed; wooden ceiling replaced by brick
MATERIALS	Local blue-gray stone
STYLE	Romanesque, Gothic

Renovation work is ongoing, particularly after the cathedral was damaged by a tornado in 1999.

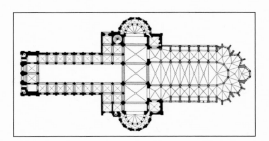

Facing page:
Tournai Cathedral as we see it today is the culmination of three different design styles ranging from the Romanesque to variations of Gothic.

Quentin Matsys's painting of St Christopher.

Brussels

BELGIUM

Cathedral of St Michael and St Gudula

The Cathedral of St Michael and St Gudula is the episcopal see of the Archbishop of Mechlin-Brussels and has headed the Catholic diocese of Brussels ever since the remains of St Gudula, daughter of a 7th-century Duke of Lotharingia, were brought to the existing church of St Michael in the 11th century. The man responsible for this was Lambert II, Duke of Brabant, who also gave the church a chapter of 12 canons. Gudula's mother had become a nun and her spiritual disposition was passed on her daughter who also achieved sainthood and is venerated, along with the archangel St Michael as patron saint of Brussels.

In the 13th century substantial renovations gave the church a Gothic makeover, and as the work continued, indulgences were granted to all who helped in the completion of the renewed building. A large 19th-century stairway leads to the three entrances. The outstanding feature inside is the stained-glass windows, a later Gothic addition, depicting the various rulers who donated them. Twelve pillars define the area of the nave, transepts, and choir, and the original foundations of the church can be seen under the crypt of the cathedral. An interesting feature is the 49-bell carillon on which Sunday concerts are given.

NAME	Cathedral of St Michael and St Gudula
ADDRESS	Parvis Ste-Gudule, 1000 Brussels, Belgium
CONSTRUCTION HISTORY	*c.* **11th century** St Michael Cathedral in existence; name changed after relics of Gudula buried here
	1226–76 Gothic choir constructed
	1450–90 West façade completed
MATERIALS	Stone
STYLE	Romanesque, Gothic

The church today is a haven for artists who are on their own spiritual journey. Thus, painters, musicians, dancers, and the like are all encouraged to meet and perform here. An annual Mass of the Artists is held in gratitude for the special gifts bestowed on these talented individuals. Royal events and state funerals are also conducted here. The 1900s were a period of continuous renovation, completed only in December 1999 in time for the wedding of the Belgian Crown Prince Philippe and Princess Mathilda.

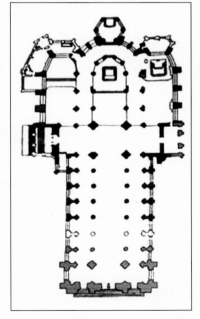

The cathedral's imposing Grenzing organ.

The stone exterior is lightened with delicate tracery on the windows and walls.

Facing page:
Belgium's leading Catholic church, the Cathedral of St Michael and St Gudula was transformed to the Gothic style from the 13th century onwards.

Ghent

Brussels

BELGIUM

St Bavo's Cathedral

The magnificent cathedral of Ghent is an expression of the wealth that this beautiful Belgian city possessed, being at the center of the Flemish cloth trade in the 11th century. The cathedral was built on the site of the 10th-century wooden Chapel of St John the Baptist. By the end of the 13th century when the Romanesque successor to the chapel started deteriorating and the need for a larger church arose, construction began on the present Gothic cathedral and continued till the 16th century. This was renamed and dedicated to St Bavo, a 7th-century nobleman who had abandoned a dissolute life to follow in the footsteps of a monk. Bavo eventually became a monk himself, living at an abbey which he built and where he died. Emperor Charles V dissolved the abbey in 1539 as a result of a rebellion, and its canons were attached to St John's church (renamed St Bavo's) and elevated to a cathedral in 1561 on the establishment of the Ghent diocese.

Not much remains of the earlier Romanesque church; only traces are visible in the crypt. The Gothic transformation continued for over 200 years until the 16th century when a new choir, chapels, the transept, nave aisles, and the single tower were added. Like the churches of its time, St Bavo's was the repository of masterpieces of art. Foremost among these is the 24-piece Ghent altarpiece, titled *The Adoration of the Mystic Lamb* by Hubert and Jan van Eyck, which achieved greater fame when several of its panels were removed and traveled back and forth during the 20th century as a fallout of the two world wars.

NAME	St Bavo's Cathedral
ADDRESS	Bisdomplein 1 Ghent 9000, Belgium
CONSTRUCTION HISTORY	**942 CE** Chapel consecrated; expanded **1038**
	End 13th / early 14th century Present cathedral begun; 1353 choir consecrated
	Early 15th century Choir chapels complete
	1462–1538 Tower built; aisles and nave begun
	1560s Cathedral consecrated
MATERIALS	Stone, brick roof
STYLE	Romanesque, Gothic, Baroque (exterior), Gothic (interior)

The cathedral's present collection of Renaissance and Baroque art dates back to the aftermath of the Iconoclasm of 1566 when much of its earlier Gothic decoration was destroyed. Owing to continuous renovation between the 14th and 16th centuries, even the funeral service of Charles V in 1558 could not be held here, although this was where he had been baptised 58 years earlier.

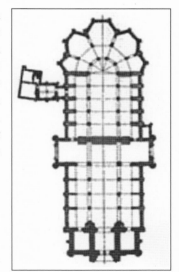

Facing page:
The awesome cathedral is the pride of Ghent city and is named after St Bavo, a reformed nobleman who achieved sainthood.

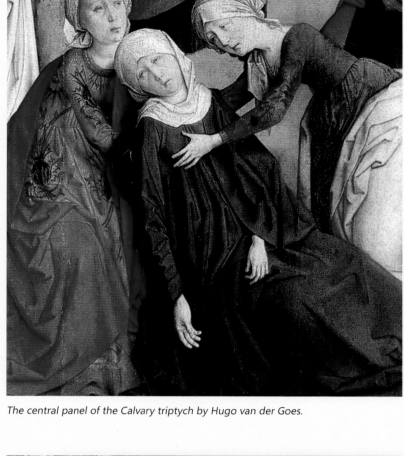

The central panel of the Calvary triptych by Hugo van der Goes.

The right panel of the Calvary triptych by Hugo van der Goes.

Cathedral of Our Lady

The Cathedral of Our Lady has been the tallest church in the Low Countries for several centuries and remains a towering landmark of Antwerp. Originally a 10th-century chapel dedicated to the Virgin Mary, it was replaced by a 12th-century Romanesque church. The present cathedral was begun in 1352 and acquired the status of a cathedral only in 1559. One hundred and seventy years in the making, a huge fire gutted the church halting completion of the south tower. A large part of the church interior was destroyed at the start of the Eighty Years' War by the Protestants, who remained in control of Antwerp until 1585 when Catholic authority was restored. It was plundered by French revolutionaries in 1794 and targeted for demolition four years later. The church lost its title of cathedral between 1801 and 1961 when bishops were deposed and church lands confiscated under the terms of the Concordat of 1801 between France and the Pope.

A truly Gothic building with delicately proportioned lines and soaring vaults, the cathedral is a repository of some of Europe's most magnificent art and sculpture. Though five towers were planned, only one was completed. Four of 17th-century Flemish painter Rubens's altarpieces were housed here; there are exquisite stained-glass windows including one depicting the Last Supper; and beautiful altars, statues, confessionals, and the pulpit. The spire was likened to the delicate Flemish lace of Mechlin by Napoleon, who took away two of Rubens's artworks to France, but which were returned in the 19th century.

NAME	Cathedral of Our Lady
ADDRESS	Handschoenmarkt (off the Grote Mkt), Antwerp, Belgium
CONSTRUCTION HISTORY	**12th century–1481** Romanesque cathedral
	1352 Construction begins of present cathedral
	1422–81 West front built; Romanesque remains completely dismantled
	1520 Cathedral complete with north tower spire built
ARCHITECTS	Jan and Pieter Appelmans, De Waghemakere (Gothic style)
MATERIALS	Stone, marble High Altar
STYLE	Gothic, Baroque

The 19th and 20th centuries have seen new additions to the church's decorative details. Restored from time to time during the 19th century, a complete restoration job took place between 1965 and 1993, which included installation of a new organ. Further extensions were added in 2005.

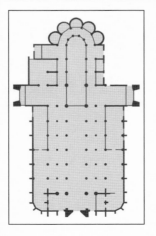

Facing page:
The completed tower of the Cathedral of Our Lady leaps upward to the spire in one of the most delicately crafted works of architecture in the world.

Gilded clock on the steeple of the cathedral.

An unlikely sculpture for a church graphically depicts its construction.

Alexander Nevsky Cathedral

UNESCO World Heritage Site

Covering an immense area of about 3000 sq m which can accommodate more than 5000 persons inside, this cathedral is named after a Russian tsar, Alexander Nevsky, who saved Russia from the invading Swedish troops in 1240. He became the patron saint of one of his successors, Alexander II, who in his turn in the late 19th century liberated Bulgaria from Ottoman rule during the Russo-Turkish War. The cathedral is dedicated to the Russian soldiers who died fighting. Sofia is one of the youngest capitals of Europe and this 100-year-old church is one of the largest Eastern Orthodox cathedrals, home of the Patriarch of Bulgaria.

The original plan for the cathedral earlier conceived was considerably altered by Pomerantsev and his colleagues. It was to be located in Tsarevets, the site of former palaces of Bulgarian royalty of the 12th–13th centuries. However, with Sofia being named the capital, the cathedral also shifted here. Money for its construction was donated by the people themselves. It follows the traditional Russian Orthodox style of multiple Byzantine half domes in weathered green copper over semi-circular apses at different heights surrounding the central main dome, largest of all. A monumental exterior with three portals rises in stepped formation to reach a tower-like form, also topped by a golden dome. Inside, there a wealth of rich decoration in Italian marble, onyx, and alabaster. Mosaics, stained-glass windows, paintings, and carvings fill the interior, while the cupola is inscribed with the prayer "Our Father" in gold letters.

NAME	St Alexander Nevsky Memorial Church
ADDRESS	Sofia, Bulgaria
CONSTRUCTION HISTORY	**1879** Foundation stone laid
	1882–1912 Cathedral built
	1924 Consecrated
COMMISSIONED BY	Constituent National Assembly in Turnovo
ARCHITECTS	Alexander Pomerantsev along with Alexander Smirnov and Alexander Yakovlev
MATERIALS	Stone, Italian marble, Brazilian onyx, alabaster
STYLE	Neo-Byzantine

For a brief period in the early 1900s the name of the cathedral was changed to the Ss Cyril and Methodius Cathedral, after two 9th-century Greek brothers who are also revered as saints in the Eastern Orthodox Church. The cathedral's crypt contains one of the finest collections of religious icons, part of the National Art Gallery of Bulgaria.

Facing page:
Alexander Nevsky Cathedral is one of the largest Eastern Orthodox cathedrals in the world.

An icon depicting Jesus and his life in the crypt of the cathedral.

Image of a saint in colorful and glittering mosaic work.

CANADA

Montreal

Ottawa

THE CITIZENS
OF
MONTREAL
GRATEFUL
1895

Montreal Notre-Dame Basilica

Preceded first by a small Jesuit chapel and then a somewhat larger church in 1657, the existing Notre-Dame in Montreal was built when it became too small for the growing laity by the beginning of the 19th century. An American architect, James O'Donnell, Irish Protestant by birth, was engaged for the job, with which he became so passionately involved that he converted to Catholicism. So far, he is the only person to be buried in the new church's crypt.

On the cathedral's structural completion in 1843 it was the largest church in the north American continent. The lavish interior took longer to be built, and each principal part was designed by different individuals. There is a bold use of colors inside. Blue is predominant on the ceiling, patterned with golden stars, while the sanctuary is a mix of reds, purples, azures and blues, gold and silver. It is further enriched by the numerous religious statues and wooden carvings that fill the space. Unusually, the stained-glass windows do not depict biblical scenes, but instead, the religious history of Montreal. Owing to its vastness, the need for an additional intimate space inside was felt, which resulted in the building of the Chapel of the Sacred Heart. This was destroyed by fire in 1978.

Dazzling gold and blue echoes the decorative style of the Sainte-Chapelle Cathedral in Paris.

NAME	Notre-Dame Basilica
ADDRESS	110 rue Notre-Dame Ouest, Montreal, QC H2Y 1T2, Canada
CONSTRUCTION HISTORY	**1672–83** Parish church built on the site; demolished 1830–43
	1824 Construction begun of present cathedral
	1843–70s First tower, High Altar, choir, pulpit completed
	1888–91 Chapelle du Sacré-Coeur built; burnt 1978; new chapel opened 1982
	1998 New altar built
ARCHITECTS	James O'Donnell, John Ostell (twin towers); Victor Bourgeau (1872–79 interior); John Redpath (stonemason); Perreault and Mesnard (Sacré-Coeur Chapel); Jodin, Lamarre, Pratte & Associates (reconstruction)
MATERIALS	Stone (from Tanneries quarry in Griffintown)
STYLE	Gothic Revival

After the chapel was burnt down it was rebuilt with the help of old drawings and photographs. A new, large bronze altarpiece, designed by Charles Daudelin, a sculptor from Quebec was now installed in it. The cathedral was raised to the status of a basilica by Pope John Paul II when he visited it in 1982. It can hold up to 4000 worshippers. The church has been the setting for significant events in modern times, most notably the funeral of Canada's 15th prime minister Pierre Trudeau. Choral and organ performances are regularly performed here.

Facing page:
A study in blue and gold, the Montreal Notre-Dame looks particularly ethereal silhouetted against the night sky.

The repetitive form of the arch is sculpted in the exterior walls with statues standing in niches defined by cusps.

St John's Basilica

Designated a basilica in 1955 by Pope Pius XII in recognition of its historical importance and artistic merits, St John's is the Roman Catholic cathedral of the diocese of St John's. Bishop Michael Anthony Fleming made five trips to England before his request for funds was granted for a piece of land where a new church could be built. The 14,000 strong Roman Catholic population of the town, largely of Irish descent, had worshipped in a small wooden church, which was fast deteriorating. Finally in 1841 the cornerstone of the new cathedral was laid. Local residents also contributed money, and both the Roman Catholic and Anglican community of the town provided the labor, led by the bishop himself, who helped quarry and load the stone, standing waist-deep in water. Progress was hampered by fire and the failure of the bank in England where the funds were kept. Fleming died soon after he held the first mass in an unfinished building, and his successor completed the structure, which included the huge two-ton St John bell that won its designer a gold medal.

The cathedral was built in the classical Romanesque style of ecclesiastical architecture, which makes it one of the earliest examples of the revival of the style in North America. It was cruciform in plan, extensive in scale, with a roof that could withstand heavy snowfall. In its time it was the largest building project of its kind in Newfoundland. Called a thoroughly Irish building, much of the statuary inside is by Irish sculptors and includes the *Dead Christ* by John Hogan. Statues of St Patrick, St Francis of Assisi, and the Immaculate Conception outside are also the work of an Irish sculptor, John Edward Carew.

The ceiling at the transept crossing is a feast for the eyes.

NAME	Basilica of John the Baptist
ADDRESS	200 Military Road, St John's, Newfoundland, Canada
CONSTRUCTION HISTORY	**1786** 1st church (wooden chapel) built
	1841 Construction begun
	1846 Damaged by fire
	1855 Building completed and consecrated
COMMISSIONED BY	Diocese of Newfoundland
ARCHITECT	John Philpot Jones, C Schmidt
MATERIALS	Stone (local), Galway limestone, Dublin granite
STYLE	Romanesque

Later additions include the 20th-century decorated ceiling and a massive organ built by the renowned firm of Casavant Frères in Quebec. The cathedral was graced by the visit of Pope John Paul II in 1984 and was given heritage status in Canada.

Facing page:
St John's was built with an outpouring of voluntary labor
from rich and poor, Anglicans and Catholics alike.

A stained-glass window picturing St John the Baptist.

Christ Church Cathedral

When Fort Victoria was established by the Hudson's Bay Company in 1843 the population was then 200. First named Victoria District Church under its chaplain, who was then succeeded by Edward Cridge, the church was later named Christ Church. The arrival of gold seekers and the rapid growth of Victoria prompted an endowment by Baroness Burdett-Coutts for a new diocese for British Columbia, and appointment of the first bishop. A new church was erected north of Christ Church, and the bishop had to choose which of the two to make the cathedral. He chose the original Christ Church, which burnt to the ground four years later. The rebuilt structure gave way to the third, present cathedral following ideological dissent between the bishop and Cridge the Dean. This resulted in Cridge's being forbidden to serve as priest of the diocese. Cridge broke away from the church, taking much of the congregation with him. Despite the reduction of parishioners Christ Church soon became too small, and a new cathedral was planned in 1891 through an international design competition.

By the time construction could start, the plan had changed somewhat. A single west tower was replaced by two smaller ones and a lantern tower added at the crossing. Limited funds, however, initially permitted building only the nave, narthex, and lower portions of the two towers, with the east end closed by a wooden wall. Eventually the plan expanded decades later to include a stone-clad two-storied addition, with chapel, Chapter House, vestries, and utility spaces. Church architecture was undergoing a change as new liturgies were being initiated, and the altar was now closer to the congregation with the clergy facing the people.

Solid stone vaulting highlighted by diffused lighting.

NAME	Christ Church Cathedral
ADDRESS	930 Burdett Avenue, Victoria, BC V8V 3G8, Canada
CONSTRUCTION HISTORY	**1853–late 1920s** 1st church built; burnt; 2nd church begun
	1929 Cathedral consecrated
	1957 Western towers built
	1980 East wall replaced by chapel, vestries, chapter room, and ancillary spaces; building complete
ARCHITECT	JCM Keith
MATERIALS	Stone
STYLE	Gothic

It took 20 years to complete the northwest bell tower, with different people donating the bells, the most recent in 1983 being dedicated by Queen Elizabeth and Prince Philip. The cathedral parish now has about 900 members.

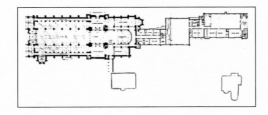

Facing page:
Designed in the Gothic Revival style, Christ Church Cathedral is a wonderful mix of an old world design with new world materials.

The stone-clad eastward extension invited 28 proposals and eventually included a chapel and offices above, and vestries and Chapter House below.

Zagreb

CROATIA

Dubrovnik

Dubrovnik Cathedral

UNESCO World Heritage Site

The picturesque port town of Dubrovnik has been inhabited since Roman times, when the first predecessor of today's Catholic cathedral stood on the same site. Its successor was a Romanesque style building, which, according to legend, was built with a donation from Richard the Lionheart, who had been shipwrecked and rescued in Dubrovnik. This 12-century church was destroyed by an earthquake in 1667, and the city elders appealed to an Italian architect Andrea Bufalini for the design of a new church. Over the next three decades, several other Italian architects contributed their ideas to make the cathedral what it is today, an exuberant Baroque edifice.

The style of the cathedral bears strong influences of Bernini, the 17th-century Italian master whose prodigious output included both sacred and secular work. The cathedral is notable for its three high naves ending in three apses and the great Baroque dome that surmounts the transept crossing. The original plan was modified by Tommaso Maria Napoli to include a cross vault and open up the windows at the upper level, thus lightening the otherwise dense interior. The cathedral is cruciform in plan, with the High Altar atypically situated at the west end. A rich array of statues of saints decorates the exterior at the level of the aisle roofs. Ornate paintings of old masters such as Titian and Andrea del Sarto enrich the interior. The cathedral's treasury contains a rich collection of about 200 reliquaries, including the gold-plated arm, leg, and skull of St Blaise, patron saint of the city. There is also a large silver cross said to enclose part of the True Cross.

Stone-carving in varied colors.

NAME	Cathedral of the Assumption
ADDRESS	Kneza Damjana Jude 1, Dubrovnik, Croatia
CONSTRUCTION HISTORY	**6th–7th century** 1st cathedral (Byzantine)
	12–14th century 2nd structure (Romanesque)
	1667 Damage by earthquake
	1670–1713 Present cathedral built
ARCHITECTS	Roman Andrea Buffalini, Paolo Andreotti
STYLE	Romanesque Baroque

During the Croation war of independence in 1991, Dubrovnik was badly bombarded. Croatia being a Catholic country, it was felt that the destruction of churches was tantamount to destruction of the main monuments of a culture. The cathedral was damaged but with UNESCO's help was soon restored to its former splendor.

Facing page:
Dubrovnik Cathedral is a three-hall building, the product of decades of expansion and renovation by many different architects.

Detail of pietra dura work on the walls.

St Vitus Cathedral

UNESCO World Heritage Site

The 'Good' King Wenceslas was a Bohemian duke who founded the original church of St Vitus in the 10th century. Intent on spreading Christianity, he is said to have acquired the arm of St Vitus as a holy relic from Henry I, hence the name. In 1060 the bishopric of Prague was established and the church expanded, replacing the original structure, which housed the tomb of St Wenceslas, who had by now become the patron saint of Czech royalty. The present cathedral was founded when it was raised to the status of an archbishopric in 1344, with Charles IV as one of its patrons. He intended to make it a coronation church, a family crypt, and a place of pilgrimage. It was designed by a Frenchman, who only lived to see the easternmost part of the choir built. On his death in 1352 the work was continued by a 23-year old German, Peter Parler, but progressed slowly.

The original Romanesque rotunda, remodeled as a triple-aisled basilica with flying buttresses and radiating chapels, was undoubtedly influenced by the original French Gothic style. Peter Parler faithfully followed this design but also introduced new elements such as the boldly patterned vaults for the choir, a dome over St Wenceslas's chapel, and a variety of sculptural ornamentation. His successors designed the Golden Gate through which kings entered the cathedral for coronation ceremonies.

NAME	St Vitus, St Wenceslas and St Adalbert Cathedral
ADDRESS	Prazsky Hrad, Prague, Czech Republic
CONSTRUCTION HISTORY	**925 CE** Church of St Vitus founded
	1060 Church expanded
	14th century Construction begins (1344); Chapel of St Wenceslas built; choir, part of transepts completed
	19th century Renovations; foundations of nave; work on façade starts, completed in 1920s
COMMISSIONED BY	King St Wenceslas (patron of original church)
ARCHITECTS	Matthias of Arras (1st master builder); Peter Parler (pillars, dome vault of chapel; architectural sculpture); Josef Kranner (restoration and interior); Josef Mocker (west façade, two towers); Kamil Hilbert (restoration)
STYLE	Gothic, Neo-Gothic

For centuries the construction was hindered by various obstacles. By the time the cathedral was finally complete, almost 600 years after its birth, a fantastic potpourri of styles had emerged. Indeed, a precedent had been set by the workshop established by Peter Parler for a style known as Late Gothic, which was to become characteristic of church architecture in Central Europe.

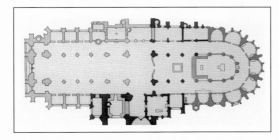

Facing page:
Located within the Prague Castle complex, St Vitus Cathedral contains the tombs of many Bohemian kings.

A sculpted detail of the wall illustrating the stems of plants and trees.

A section of the extraordinarily bold stained-glass windows depicting saints.

Roskilde Cathedral

The oldest Gothic cathedral in Denmark, Roskilde, on the island of Zealand, is considered the most important ecclesiastical building in the country. Situated in the former Danish capital, it was built on the site of a wooden church dedicated to the Holy Trinity, attributed to King Harold Bluetooth. Around 991 CE Roskilde became the seat of the bishop, and almost 100 years later, with donations from King Canute's sister, the first stone church was completed, which, until the 20th century was the national cathedral of Denmark, when it was superseded by Our Lady Church in Copenhagen. From the 15th century onwards it has been the main burial site for Danish rulers, gradually expanding its count of memorial chapels with the passage of time. Around 1540 the Catholic cathedral was forced to suspend services, and its properties were appropriated by the Crown due to the spread of Lutheranism. Roskilde was saved from vandalism because it was a royal resting place. The bishop's residence moved to Copenhagen and he held the title of Bishop of Zealand.

After a period of decline when the change to Protestant authority took place, both the structure and interior underwent some transformation. A beautiful altarpiece and pulpit were added; the west towers were raised; and the spires clad in copper. A new chapel replaced two older ones. Roskilde was the first Gothic cathedral to be entirely built in brick, and inspired a new genre of brick construction in north Europe. Most spectacular are the chapels of the monarchs, extravagantly painted and decorated, and a treasure house of artefacts.

NAME	Roskilde Cathedral (Roskilde Domkirke)
ADDRESS	Domkirkepladsen 3, 4000 Roskilde, Denmark
CONSTRUCTION HISTORY	**980–1080** 1st wooden church; 1st stone cathedral
	1170–1280 Present cathedral built and consecrated
	1310 Lady Chapel built
	1600–14 Two west towers, Christian IV's chapel built
	19th/20th century Restoration
MATERIALS	Brick, wooden choir stalls
STYLE	Romanesque, Gothic

Among the royalty that lies buried in the eleven chapels, crypt, and hall outside the cathedral, are Frederick IX (1899–1972) and Ingrid Bernadotte, Princess of Sweden (1910–2000). The Royal Column records the height of visiting princes—Edward VII of England, Peter the Great of Russia, and the Thai king, Chulalongkorn.

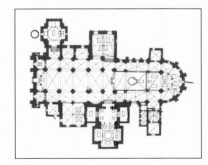

Facing page:
The twin towers of Roskilde, clad in copper, soar upwards in colorful contrast to the brick structure of the rest of the cathedral.

A glittering High Altar stands out against the backdrop of the brick walls.

The bright imagery of a star-spangled sky highlights sections of the ceiling.

Salisbury Cathedral

Towering magnificently above its picturesque surroundings, Salisbury Cathedral superbly exemplifies the harmony of built form and nature. Built by St Osmond, the church started as a Norman cathedral on higher ground at Old Sarum but was damaged by exposure to winds and lightning. In 1215 Bishop Richard le Poore shifted its location, and a few years later construction of the Gothic cathedral began. As it was enlarged part by part, starting with the east end, the church could only be considered complete when the spire, its most striking feature, was completed almost 100 years later. The cathedral is home to one of the best preserved extant copies of the *Magna Carta* and also to Europe's oldest working clock, dating from the 14th century.

A unique homogeneity and simplicity of style make this one of the most enduring and easily intelligible of medieval cathedrals. A series of rectangular units with their own mini-spires build up to the central spire, the tallest in England and a work of engineering ingenuity. The cloisters, also the largest in England, were used as a prison during the 17th-century Civil War. The octagonal Chapter House is a fine example of the Geometrical Decorated style. The earliest part of the building is the enchanting Lady Chapel where three bishops, including St Osmond, are entombed. Remedial structural elements, such as the flying buttresses outside, internal buttresses, and reinforcing arches and a lierne vault underneath the steeple, became necessary when the 4200-ton spire was erected, but they do not disturb the essential clarity of the design.

The cloisters are distinguished by bold floral tracery on the walls, open on one side and blind on the other.

NAME	The Cathedral Church of the Blessed Virgin Mary
ADDRESS	6 The Close, Salisbury, Wiltshire SP1 2EF, UK
CONSTRUCTION HISTORY	**1075** 1st Norman cathedral begun
	1220 Gothic cathedral begun
	13th century Chapel of the Holy Trinity and All Saints, choir, transepts, nave, west front, cloister, Chapter House built; consecrated 1258
	14th century Tower and spire built
	18th/19th century 1st and 2nd restoration
COMMISSIONED BY	Bishop Richard le Poore
ARCHITECTS	Nicholas of Ely (master mason); Elias of Dereham (craftsman)
MATERIALS	Chilmark stone, Purbeck marble, oak choir stalls, lead roof covering
STYLE	Early English Gothic, Geometrical Decorated (Chapter House)

Two major renovations have occurred--James Wyatt's in the 18th century, and George Gilbert Scott's in the 19th century, the latter attempting to restore some of the church's original aesthetics. The cathedral close includes some interesting examples of domestic architecture and several educational institutions.

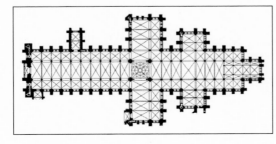

Facing page:
Salisbury's plan consists of a series of rectangular blocks culminating in the magnificent spire rising to a height of 404 ft (123 m).

The balance of vertical and horizontal lines is emphasized by the use of contrasting colors of Purbeck marble as in this section looking east.

London
Canterbury

Canterbury Cathedral

Canterbury Cathedral is the foremost Anglican church in the world. Its first archbishop was Augustine of Canterbury, sent by Pope Gregory in 597 CE to spread the faith in England. His base was St Martin's Church at Canterbury, still in use. When ordained bishop, he established the cathedral. The original church, which was part of the Benedictine monastery, was thoroughly rebuilt by Archbishop Lanfranc by 1077 and though its monastic connections were dissolved in 1540 it continued as a house of prayer. The cathedral was made famous by the murder and almost immediate canonization of Archbishop Thomas Becket, who was murdered inside it in 1170 when he switched allegiance from King Henry II to the Pope. Henry, who almost immediately repented, became one of the first flock of pilgrims to worship at Becket's shrine.

The cathedral's most spectacular rebuilding took place after it burned down in 1174. The French architect William of Sens redesigned the eastern end, working within the constraints set by the monks that it should retain as much of its burnt-out shell as possible. The alteration is distinctively French Gothic in style. The work had to be completed by William (he Englishman). He designed the Trinity Chapel and Corona, perhaps the most splendid part of the interior, in marble of varied colors, 'miracle' stained-glass windows, and also renovated the arcade.

NAME	Cathedral and Metropolitical Church of Christ at Canterbury
ADDRESS	The Precincts, Canterbury, Kent CT1 2EH, UK
CONSTRUCTION HISTORY	*c.* **1077** Church of the Benedictine monastery rebuilt
	12th century Church burnt down; choir rebuilt; eastern crypt, Trinity and Corona chapels added
	14th–15th century New nave and cloister vaulted; southwest tower, pulpitum screen, Bell Harry Tower added
	17th–19th century repair and refurbishing; northwest tower rebuilt
ARCHITECTS	William of Sens (1184); William (the Englishman); John Wastell (Bell Harry Tower); Henry Yevele (14th century)
MATERIALS	Caen stone, brick, Purbeck marble
STYLE	Gothic

The Civil War and Restoration in the 17th century exacted their toll of the building. Right up to the 19th century large-scale remodeling took place. The cathedral was saved from disaster during World War II thanks to the vigilance of fire fighters. Outside its walled precincts an ancient monastery now houses the King's School. There are also several canonical gardens, including a modern-day Herbarium.

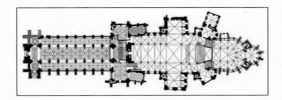

Facing page:
England's premier cathedral when illuminated looks especially magnificent.

Stained-glass windows depict scenes from the life of Christ, miraculous cures, and figures of kings and archbishops.

At Canterbury, as elsewhere, the Eucharist was central to the faith.

Winchester Cathedral

Winchester, which began as the Priory of St Swithun, is one of England's great cathedrals. It houses the relics of Saxon kings, the Viking King Canute, Alfred the Great and William the Conqueror. The 18th-century novelist Jane Austen is also buried here. The Benedictine monk Swithun was bishop of Winchester and King Alfred's tutor. According to his wishes, he was first buried outside the building so that "the rain from the eaves may fall on my grave," but his remains were moved inside when the abbey was enlarged in 971 CE, and later to the new Norman cathedral of 1079. The church was remodeled several times by the powerful bishops of the diocese. Its final reconstruction appropriated the Gothic vocabulary, and the Perpendicular Gothic nave, an outstanding feature, is reputed to be one of the longest in England.

Only the crypt, transepts, and crossing tower survive from Norman times. The crypt, where the remains of St Swithun lie, still floods every winter despite an extraordinary effort at concrete reshoring undertaken in the 20th century with the help of divers. Under Bishop Wykeham, a great patron of the arts, the original nave was refashioned. Extension of the east end in the 13th century included the retrochoir, a particularly interesting part of the church. Here stand the chantry chapels of three bishops, each outdoing the other in lavishness. The western façade has a huge window surmounting Perpendicular style arches in the porch.

NAME	Cathedral Church of the Holy Trinity, and of St Peter and St Paul and of St Swithun
ADDRESS	9 The Close, Winchester, Hampshire, SO23 9LS, UK
CONSTRUCTION HISTORY	**648 CE** 1st Saxon church
	1079 Present Norman cathedral begun
	13th century East end expanded
	c. 1400 Gothic nave remodeled; west front, choir stalls built
COMMISSIONED BY	1079 foundations laid by Bishop Walkelin
MATERIALS	Stone from Isle of Wight, oak from Hampshire
STYLE	Norman, Romanesque

In the 19th century, an eye-catching limestone screen was recarved with figures of Saxon bishops and monarchs, which strangely includes Queen Victoria. A haunting modern-day sculpture stands unharmed when flooding takes place in the crypt. The cathedral has had bells since the Saxon period and boasts the only diatonic ring of 14 in the world.

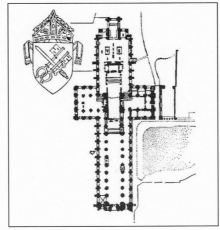

A fascinating network of ribs decorates the vaulted ceiling, brightly lit through clerestory windows on the uppermost level.

The chantry chapels of Winchester are famous, with colorful images of saints sculpted in decorative niches.

Facing page:
Winchester was at the heart of a powerful diocese that stretched from the River Thames to the Channel Islands.

Ely Cathedral

Ely Cathedral was an old church that was restored by St Etheldreda, daughter of a Saxon king, who received the Isle of Ely as dowry on her first marriage. Although married twice, she remained a virgin and fled to Ely when pressurized to consummate her second marriage. Along with the church, Etheldreda also founded a monastery in 673 CE. Burnt and pillaged by Danes 200 years later, both were rebuilt in the 10th century, and St Etheldreda's shrine became a major source of pilgrimage revenue. King Canute is said to have been a frequent visitor. Today's church was built by the Normans under Abbot Simeon, a relative of William the Conqueror, when it also became a cathedral (in 1109).

Called the 'Ship of the Fens', because it stands out above the marshy landscape, the cathedral's oldest parts are the 12th-century undercroft and part of the infirmary building. Most of it was completed in the 13th century, extended, and remodeled until it was dismantled by Henry VIII, and then rebuilt. The exterior is a work of ornamental exuberance, unmatched by the comparatively less decorative four-level interior, which is covered with blind arcades. Ely possesses one of the longest naves in England. The stone walls highlight the painted timber ceiling. When the original central tower at the crossing collapsed, it was replaced by an unusual octagonal lantern-tower of striking elegance.

NAME	Cathedral Church of the Holy and Undivided Trinity
ADDRESS	The College, Ely, Cambridgeshire CB7 4DL, UK
CONSTRUCTION HISTORY	**1083** Construction begun
	1174–97 West tower built
	14th century Lady Chapel built; central tower falls
	1539 Cathedral closed down; refounded as a 'New' cathedral in 1541
MATERIALS	Stone, marble and local clunch, timber-roofed nave
STYLE	Norman, Romanesque, Early English/Gothic/Victorian renovations

Ely Cathedral suffered less under King Henry VIII's Reformation than other monasteries, being refounded in 1541. It also escaped the full thrust of Cromwell's ire although he shut it down for 11 years. Under architect George Gilbert Scott the church was finally restored to its full glory in the 19th century, and conservation work is ongoing. A national Stained Glass Museum is one of its main attractions.

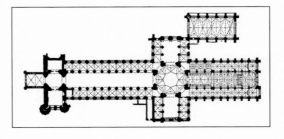

One of the twelve painted panels on the nave ceiling.

Wooden triangles support the Gothic dome in the lantern-tower.

Facing page:
Ely Cathedral, with its octagonal lantern-tower, dominates the small town and the surrounding Fens.

Durham Cathedral

The history of Durham Cathedral recalls the life of St Cuthbert, the beloved 7th-century bishop of the Benedictine monastery of Lindisfarne. Two hundred years after his death, in the face of Viking invasions, the monks of the abbey had to flee with his relics, and finally settled down above the river Wear in 995 CE. The first church, a wooden structure made to house St Cuthbert's relics, was replaced by a stone structure called the White Church. The present cathedral is the third structure to have been built here, and resulted from the intense building activity that followed the Norman invasion of England. It was a place of pilgrimage and also served a political function, reinforcing the authority of the prince-bishops in northern England. The Reformation brought about the dissolution of the monastic community and destruction of many artefacts, including St Cuthbert's tomb. It was later reinstated and placed under a stone slab behind the High Altar.

The cathedral developed piecemeal until the 15th century and is typical of the large-scale, heavy buildings of the Norman Romanesque style. It contains the first English example of rib vaulting being used throughout the building, which, along with the skilled use of the pointed arch, enabled larger, more complex spaces to be covered. The interior is three-storied, the uppermost level being a clerestory gallery.

NAME	Cathedral Church of Christ, Blessed Mary the Virgin and St Cuthbert of Durham
ADDRESS	The College, Durham DH1 3EQ, UK
CONSTRUCTION HISTORY	**1093–1133** Choir, transepts, nave built; consecrated 1133
	1170–75 Galilee Chapel built
	13th century Western towers completed; Chapel of Nine Altars built
	1465–90 Central tower completed
COMMISSIONED BY	William of Calais; Bishop Hugh de Puiset (1170s Galilee Chapel); Richard le Poore (1228 Chapel of Nine Altars)
ARCHITECTS	Richard Farnham (13th-century Chapel of Nine Altars); Thomas Barton, John Bell (master masons of the 13th-century central tower)
MATERIALS	Stone
STYLE	Norman, Romanesque

During the late 18th century a significant amount of the stone exterior was chiseled off. Restoration work continues to date, funded by the cathedral itself, and includes the upkeep of the beautiful river banks on which the building is located. Durham University owes its founding to the first endowments gifted by the cathedral bishop and chapter in 1882. Today, all university degrees are conferred inside the cathedral.

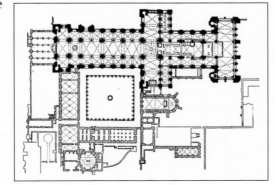

Facing page:
The cathedral stands on a rock face high above the river Wear.

View of the cathedral from the cloisters.

The Great West Doorway.

Gloucester Cathedral

Formerly in St Peter's Abbey, this church did not become a cathedral until 1541, when Henry VIII declared it as such. Originally built in wood over Roman foundations by the Saxon king Osric in 681 CE, it was by the 9th century rebuilt in stone. A grander rebuilding took place in the mid 11th century at the behest of the Bishop of Worcester, but towards the end of the century the structure was destroyed by fire. Before this, it had achieved fame by being the place from where William the Conqueror had ordered the great survey of England, compiled as the Doomsday Book. The boy king Henry III was crowned here, and in 1330 the murdered King Edward II was buried at this site, both events attracting enough interest in the church to draw substantial revenue for its upkeep. The martyred Edward's shrine protected the church from destruction at the dissolution of the monasteries. Notwithstanding Cromwell's attempts to demolish the cathedral in the mid 17th century, normalcy was restored under Charles II in 1660.

The cathedral best exemplifies the Perpendicular style, where curved lines are eliminated through the arrangement of windows in a rectangle, and this element becomes a prominent decorative motif. In contrast to a predilection for greater simplicity than had thus far been the convention, the roofing presents a bewildering jumble of ribs of all possible types, camouflaging the Norman barrel vault. Notable are the monuments to Osric and Edward II (in alabaster), and the 14th-century cloisters, but most striking is the Great East Window, which displays religious imagery of superb quality.

NAME	Cathedral Church of the Holy and Indivisible Trinity
ADDRESS	12 College Green, Gloucester GL1 2LX, UK
CONSTRUCTION HISTORY	**681 CE** Abbey church built in wood
	9th century Stone replacement
	1089- 1337 Burnt down; main building rebuilt
	1100 Consecrated
	1541 Declared cathedral by Henry VIII
COMMISSIONED BY	Abbot Serlo
MATERIALS	Stone
STYLE	Norman, Romanesque, Gothic

Like all famous cathedrals, Gloucester was remodeled and built upon several times in medieval times. The later 19th century saw extensive restoration work by the architect George Gilbert Scott. The Chapter House of the church is now used as an examination room by the neighboring King's School, while parts of the building have been imaginatively used for a Harry Potter film.

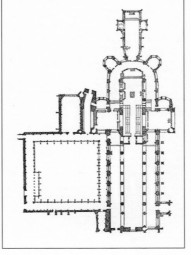

Facing page:
Gloucester Cathedral grew from a Norman abbey church and demonstrates a wealth of shapes and details.

The cloister echoes the basic vaulting pattern of the rest of the church while retaining as much of the original structure as possible.

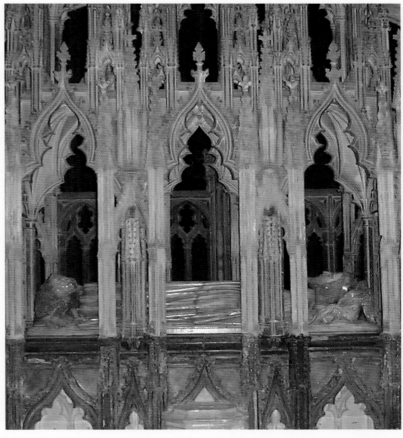

Vertical lines and elongated cusped arches create one of the first examples of the Perpendicular style.

ENGLAND

London

Wells

Wells Cathedral

Competing with Glastonbury and Bath for the bishopric, Wells emerged the winner in the 13th century. Bishop Jocelyn directed most of the construction of the cathedral, but by the time the early phase of building was over, the laity had grown so large as to necessitate further expansion. Fourteenth-century master mason Thomas of Witney was responsible for the Chapter House and Lady Chapel, two of its most beautiful parts. By the reign of Henry VII the cathedral was largely complete. The dissolution of the monasteries reduced the income of the church and it was forced to sell off some of its treasures. Subsequent events also caused considerable neglect and damage to the cathedral: the English Civil War, when the clergy was reduced to penury, the Puritan rebellion of 1685, and the great storm of 1703.

Several bishops supervised additions and changes, but the existing dynamism of the Gothic style goes back to the early 14th century. The octagonal Chapter House, with a richly decorated vault and mesh of mushrooming pillars circling around the central one is breathtaking. Another unique feature is the elongated octagonal Lady Chapel, the only one of its kind in England. It connects with the rectangular ambulatory around the choir, using another geometric form, the hexagon. Wells's masterpiece is however its gigantic western screen façade with life-sized figures of saints and secular figures on top of which Christ sits at the Last Judgment.

NAME	Cathedral Church of St Andrew
ADDRESS	Chain Gate, Cathedral Green, Wells, Somerset BA5 2UE, UK
CONSTRUCTION HISTORY	**705 CE** 1st church built
	1180/90 2nd church begun; consecrated c. 1240
	14th century Chapter House; Lady Chapel built
	1400 Towers complete
COMMISSIONED BY	King Ine of Wessex (1st church); Bishop Reginald de Bohun, Bishop Jocelyn of Wells, Bishop John Drokensford (present cathedral)
ARCHITECTS	Elias of Dereham, Thomas of Witney, William Joy, William Wynford (master masons)
MATERIALS	Yellow oolite, Purbeck marble
STYLE	Early English Gothic, Geometrical Decorated (new choir)

In an operation known as the "great scrape" a major restoration program was undertaken in the middle of the 19th century, when remnants of the medieval era whitewash were removed and monuments shifted to the cloisters. Many of the Christian images that were most accessible in the lower areas had been stolen or destroyed during iconoclastic episodes of English history.

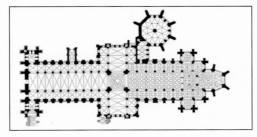

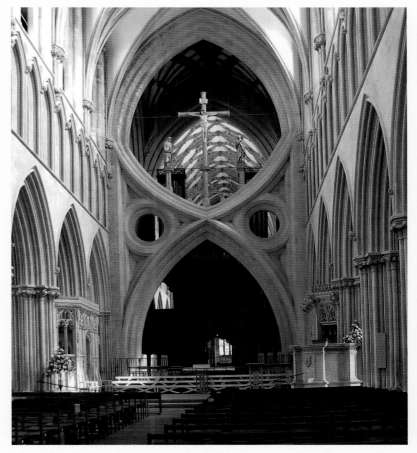

The unique inverted arch was a daring solution found to support the central tower at the crossing when the building was enlarged and the spire added.

Unlikely imagery of one man hitting another, a man with a toothache, a thorn extractor, and others are seen on the capitals in the southwest arm of the transept.

Facing page:
Wells has been described as "the most poetic of English cathedrals" and has a splendid Early English façade.

ENGLAND

Lincoln

London

Lincoln Cathedral

This Norman cathedral was reputed to exceed the height of the Great Pyramid at Giza for about 200 years, thus making it the world's tallest structure until its spire collapsed in a storm in 1549. The present towers of Lincoln Cathedral were built by Bishop Remegius when the diocese shifted from Dorchester to Lincoln, on the site of a mother church. A further expansion occurred 50 years later, but was destroyed by an earthquake, and its only surviving features are to be found in parts of the west front and towers. The first rebuilding of the church was done with stones from part of the town wall, with King Henry III's permission.

Fortress-like in appearance when built by the Normans, the later Gothic changes incorporated the full language of pointed arches, ribbed vaulting, flying buttresses, and huge stained-glass windows, which provided a model for later churches. However, owing to the experimental use of early Gothic there have been continual problems with various parts of the structure. Following the example of Canterbury there was also a double transept. The use of Purbeck marble accentuates the horizontality of the interior space. The cathedral has Europe's first recorded star vault based on the patterning of the ribs. The focus of building shifted to memorial chapels in the 15th century as part of the cathedral.

NAME	Cathedral Church of St Mary in Lincoln
ADDRESS	The Chapter, 4 Priorygate, Lincoln, LN2 1PL, UK
CONSTRUCTION HISTORY	**1072–92** 1st church built and consecrated in 1092; burnt and destroyed by earthquake
	1192 Present church begun, completed 1280
	13th century Central tower collapses; rebuilding begins
	14th century Central tower and spire, pulpitum, St Hugh's Choir built
	1549 East end enlarged
COMMISSIONED BY	William the Conqueror
MATERIALS	Limestone, stone, Purbeck marble
STYLE	Gothic, Romanesque, chapels in Perpendicular Gothic

The cathedral possesses one of the four extant copies of the *Magna Carta* and also a 1410 schoolbook with the first recorded rhyme on Robin Hood. In the past, each expansion and rebuilding of the church involved changes to the east end. The tower and spire have had to be continually shored up and restored, and today over one million pounds are spent each year for conservation of the cathedral.

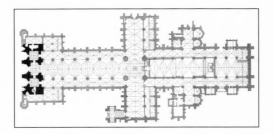

Facing page:
Towering above its surroundings, Lincoln Cathedral presents a vocabulary of diverse architectural forms that were used for the first time in England.

A sculpted gallery of kings surmounts the lavish entrance gateway to the cathedral.

In the remodeling of several early cathedrals, the flying buttress became a necessary external support.

Westminster Abbey

UNESCO World Heritage Site

Westminster Abbey is the resting place of England's most famous poets, musicians, scientists, and politicians, as well as 17 of its monarchs. Until the 19th century it was the most important seat of learning in England after Oxford and Cambridge. The abbey was supposedly built by Edward the Confessor at the suggestion of the Pope that he redeem himself for failing to go on a promised pilgrimage. In 1066, William the Conqueror was crowned here, setting a royal tradition whereby Westminster Abbey became popularly known as the coronation church. It also became a center for pilgrimage after it housed the shrine of Edward. The present grand edifice was built by Henry III. Between 1540–60 it held the status of a cathedral. Its royal connections saved it from destruction, and ultimately it was restored as a collegiate church and a Royal Peculiar by Elizabeth I in 1560.

Henry III's architects designed Westminster on the French Gothic models of Reims, Amiens, and Chartres. The plan retained the English long, narrow nave and wide projecting transepts but incorporated the idea of the apse with radiating chapels. The nave vault is the highest in England. A wide space between the High Altar and choir provides a dramatic setting for coronations to take place. Among the chapels, the new 16th-century Lady Chapel is the most beautiful, bearing 100 statues of saints and stone carvings on the surrounding walls. Geoffrey Chaucer, a tenant on the Abbey grounds is buried in a section now known as Poets' Corner.

NAME	Collegiate Church of St Peter at Westminster
ADDRESS	20 Dean's Yard, Westminster, London SW1P 3PA, UK
CONSTRUCTION HISTORY	**1050** Romanesque Abbey church built; replaced later by Norman church
	1245 Present Gothic church begun by Henry III
	1375 New nave built by Richard II
	1503–19 Chapels built, including Lady Chapel
	1745 Gothic Revival west towers built
COMMISSIONED BY	Edward the Confessor (1st church); Henry III
ARCHITECTS	Henry of Reyns, John of Gloucester, Robert of Beverley (13th-century), Henry Yevele (14th century); John Thirske (15th century); Robert Janyns, William Vertue (new Lady Chapel); Nicholas Hawksmoor (west towers)
MATERIALS	Stone from Caen (France) and Reigate in Surrey (UK), Portland stone
STYLE	Gothic

Fortunately the church escaped major damage during World War II, and it was here that the New English Bible was compiled in 1961 (in the same Deanery where the Authorized Version of the King James Bible had been put together in 1611).

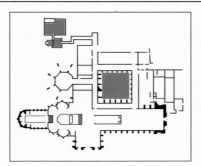

Sculpted tympanum of Westminster Cathedral depicts the central figure of Christ in Majesty being revered.

King Edward's Chair also housed the Stone of Scone on which the kings of Scotland were crowned; the Stone is now housed in Scotland.

Facing page:
Perhaps the most famous of English churches, Westminster Abbey, designated a Royal Peculiar, has been England's coronation church since 1066.

ENGLAND

Exeter   London

Exeter Cathedral

The foundations of a large Saxon church, believed to be the first home of Exeter Cathedral, were discovered in 1970 when the nearby Victorian church of St Mary Major was demolished. This was probably the Saxon minster of the seventh century, dedicated to St Mary and St Peter. It became the seat of the bishop of Devon and Cornwall when the region was threatened by attacks from the sea. Its Norman style replacement was begun in the 12th century, but for no obvious reason, extensive rebuilding took place 100 years later. Supposedly, successive bishops wishing to enhance its architectural beauty were responsible for the next Gothic transformation, which took almost a century to be realized. The design of the first cathedral was inspired by the nearby example at Salisbury.

Exeter bears the distinction of having the longest uninterrupted Gothic ceiling in the world. Its most original feature, striking in its architectonics, is the vaulting and articulation of the bays. A series of engaged columns run along the three-tiered nave, from which, at the second level, the ribs spread out towards the center of the ceiling. In plan, the cathedral follows the early Gothic style with double transepts and a flat-ended choir. The towers constitute the major survivors of the Norman building; their internal walls were later replaced by arches leading to the transepts, with large Gothic windows. A beautiful pulpit screen separates the worshippers from the area designated for priests. An unusual feature of the cathedral is the "green men"—carvings of men or animals with foliage emanating from their mouths, ears, or noses, or surrounded by it.

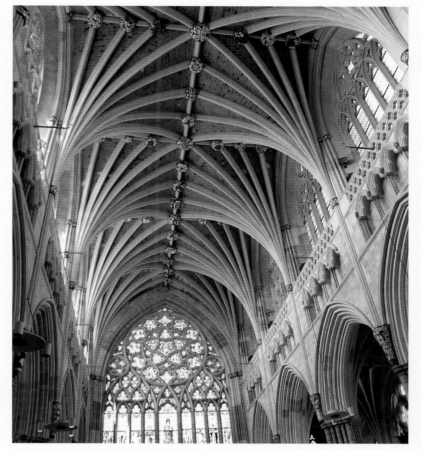

Ribs blossom forth from piers on either side of the three-tiered nave to meet in the center of the ceiling.

NAME	Cathedral Church of St Peter in Exeter
ADDRESS	1 The Cloisters, Exeter, EX1 1HS, UK
CONSTRUCTION HISTORY	**1114–1170/80** Norman cathedral; consecrated 1133
	1265/70 Gothic rebuilding begun
	14th century Body of cathedral complete
COMMISSIONED BY	Bishop William Warelwast
MATERIALS	Stone, Sicilian marble font, oak canopy over cathedra
STYLE	Gothic, Romanesque

In the demolition process that took place in the 1970s, a number of cemeteries were excavated in the northern part of the site. Traditionally, this was the only place from ancient times to the mid 17th century where burials were allowed in Exeter.

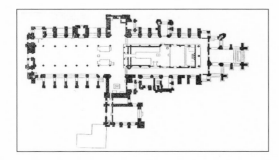

Facing page:
Exeter Cathedral's blind and sculptured screen façade was typical of the Gothic style in England.

An ornate, gilded tomb of one of the cathedral's past bishops.

St Paul's Cathedral

Long before the advent of Christianity in England, Ludgate Hill was a sacred site, where the Romans had built a temple to the goddess Diana. The first church was built over the temple ruins in the early 7th century. The present cathedral is the fourth church built here. Its predecessor, Old St Paul's, took over 300 years to complete, with a new west front added to it by Inigo Jones, England's first classical architect. For centuries public meetings were held and important announcements made inside, where gradually a market place emerged. Its final debasement was at the hands of Oliver Cromwell, who used it for his cavalry during the Civil War between Parliament and king. Devastation by the Great Fire of London in 1666 provided the opportunity to architect Christopher Wren to realize his dream for a new design, which he had proposed three years earlier.

Though Wren's original grand plan was toned down, the magnificent dome echoes that of St Peter's in Rome and is embellished with frescoes inside. Over the years numerous plaques, carvings, and monuments commemorating well-known members of the laity, clergy, and the British military have enhanced the interior. Among these are a memorial to Florence Nightingale. There are three small chapels, and a large one in the crypt. Of the three galleries, the Whispering Gallery is famous for its unique acoustics. The Stone and Golden galleries offer panoramic views of London. Highlights include the cathedral's great organ and the wrought-ironwork by Jean Tijou in 1700.

A vaulted arcade inside the cathedral.

NAME	Cathedral Church of St Paul the Apostle
ADDRESS	Ludgate Hill EC4, The City, London, UK
CONSTRUCTION HISTORY	**7th century CE** 1st and 2nd churches
	c. **1088–1314** 3rd church (Old St Paul's)
	1666 Old St Paul's burnt down by Great Fire of London
	1675–1708 Present cathedral built; consecrated 1708
	2000 Restoration program begun
ARCHITECT	Christopher Wren
MATERIALS	Stone
STYLE	Neo-Classical, English Baroque

Nelson and the Duke of Wellington are among those to have been buried here in the 19th century, while royal family marriages and anniversaries have been held here in more recent history. Most of the cathedral survived World War II, and a part behind the High Altar was rebuilt as a chapel to honor Americans who gave their lives in the war effort. In 2000 a restoration program costing £40 million was begun to celebrate its 300th anniversary, and this includes upgraded visitor facilities.

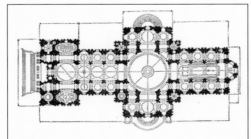

Facing page:
The final resting place of heroes, St Paul's has been a spiritual center of England for centuries.

Detail of the exterior columns with decorated capitals.

Helsinki Cathedral

Much before the first cathedral was built on this site, some say there was a smaller church dedicated to and named after its patron Ulrika Eleonora, the 18th-century Queen of Sweden. However, the first recorded cathedral on this site is the one built as a tribute to the Tsar of Russia, Nicholas I, and named after him until the independence of Finland in 1917. Dominating the Senate Square where it stands, it was designed in a style similar to the other surrounding buildings by the same architect and replaced the earlier church of 1727. It was only in 1959 that the church became a cathedral of the Evangelical Lutheran denomination. A landmark of Helsinki, easily identified because of its towering green domes, it is as popular with worshippers as it is with tourists.

The four towers and their domes were added by Engels's successor, Ernst Lohrmann, after Engels died. Lohrmann also added a belfry and chapel and, most noticeably, the larger than life-size statues of the Apostles on the roof. According to some, the Neo-Classical style of the cathedral harks back to Greek and Rome, and to others, to Saint Isaac's Cathedral in St Petersburg. It was built on the Greek cross plan with four arms of equal length, and each symmetrically designed with a colonnade and pediment. The interior is without excessive flourishes, with handsome proportions. Engel also created the statues of angels on both sides of the altarpiece and pulpit, but his original overall design was somewhat altered by later architectural additions by his successor to resonate more clearly with the St Petersburg model.

Statues of saints, decorative capitals, and star-spangled copper domes are highlighted by the plastered white exterior.

NAME	Lutheran Cathedral (Tuomiokirkko), White Cathedral, Helsinki Cathedral, St Nicholas' Church
ADDRESS	Senate Square, Helsinki, Finland
CONSTRUCTION HISTORY	**1727** Earlier church
	1830–52 Present cathedral constructed; bell towers, side chapel, four domes added
	1980s–98 Crypt renovated; conservation work
ARCHITECTS	Carl Ludvig Engel; Ernst Lohrmann; Vilhelm Helander and Juha Leiviskä (crypt, conservation)
MATERIALS	Stone, zinc statues on roof
STYLE	Neo-Classical

The crypt, which some find gloomy but atmospheric, was renovated in the 1980s to house a café and to be used for exhibitions and church functions. Further renovations were carried out in the 1990s.

The clock is embedded in the main tower.

Facing page:
The Lutheran Cathedral and the Senate Square in which it stands echo the severe Neo-Classical style of ancient Greece and Rome.

Rock Church

Designed by two architect brothers, the Lutheran Rock Church in Helsinki is one of the landmarks of modern church architecture. Built in the heart of the city, the location had been selected in the 1930s and a design was chosen through a competition. Construction was delayed due to the onset of World War II in 1939. Another competition was held after the war ended, and won by two architect brothers, who devised the ingenious plan of excavating a 40-ft (9 m) high rock face and building within it and underground so that the original character of the location remained. On the surface there would only be visible the cone-shaped copper dome, like a huge flying saucer. Owing to its innovative design, the project was held up for almost nine years by negative propaganda. It was eventually built after paring down a large part of the congregational space.

Oval in plan and enclosed within a meandering bare granite wall, natural light obtains from 180 vertical window panes connecting the glazed dome and the wall. The incredibly spartan interior can be viewed from above, from a copper colored balcony. It is a single hall with seating arranged in a semi-circle divided by aisles. There is no tower, and therefore a recording of bells, specially composed, is transmitted through loudspeakers. A dramatic rock face provides the backdrop for the organ and serves as the wall behind the altar. The color scheme is based on shades of granite-red, purple, and gray, but perhaps the most spectacular feature is the gleaming ceiling netted together with copper wires.

NAME	Rock Church or Church of the Rock (Temppeliaukio Kirkko)
ADDRESS	Lutherinkatu 3, SF-00100 Helsinki, Finland
CONSTRUCTION HISTORY	1968–69; consecrated 1969
ARCHITECTS	Timo and Tuomo Suomalainen
MATERIALS	Granite, copper ceiling and dome
STYLE	Modern

The rock surfaces make for excellent acoustics, in virtue of which the church is popularly used for concerts of sacred music. The church has become one of Helsinki's major attractions, both for its architecture and classical concerts, and services are held every Sunday afternoon in English.

Church organ seen from the balcony.

The underside of the roof is a mesh of copper wires.

Facing page:
Emerging like a flying saucer from the ground in which it is embedded, the Rock Church is a masterpiece of modern design.

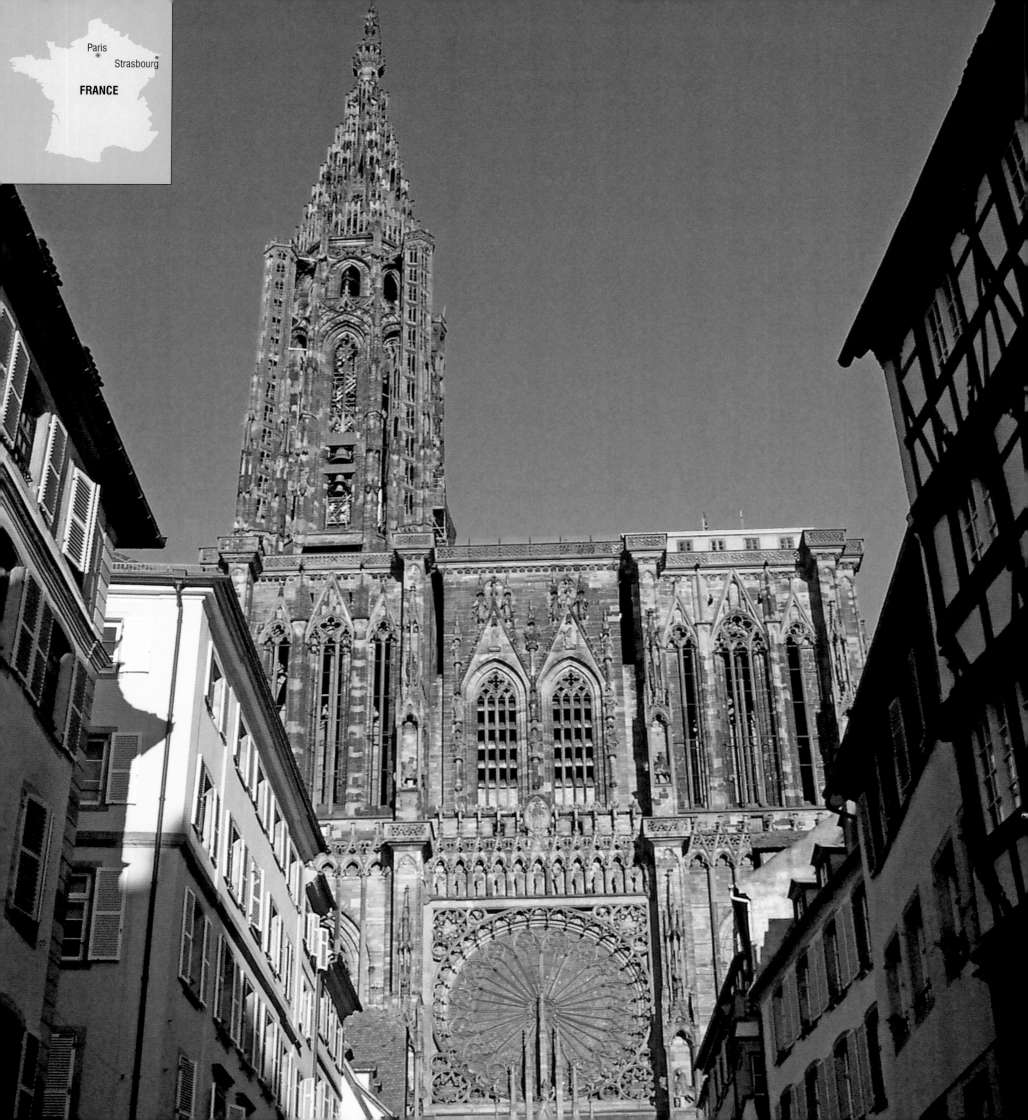

Strasbourg Cathedral

At least two religious buildings preceded the present cathedral, which stands on the site of a forum in the ancient Roman town of Argentoratum. The remains of the first (4th–5th century) cathedral were excavated in 1948 and 1956. The second cathedral, built in the 8th century, contains the crypt of Bishop Remigius von Strasbourg. It was on the ruins of this Carolingian cathedral, damaged by fire at least three times, that the present cathedral stands, its predecessor having been burned to the ground in 1176. As always, the crypt, being underground, was a natural survivor, and from this starting point, the new building expanded westwards.

Strasbourg Cathedral creates an overarching impression of height by its screen of steeply pointed gables and the arcades and vertical forms that cover the entire surface of the façade. Two styles are distinct in the cathedral. The Romanesque, in which the earliest sections, the choir and the north transept were made, and the Gothic, introduced by a new master mason presumably from Chartres, around 1225. The two, however, combine seamlessly. Gradually, the apse, south transept, choir screen, and vaults were built. About 50 years later, work started on the west façade under the expert hand of Erwin von Steinbach. This is one of the earliest façades, which is said to have made use of architectural drawings. The nave has unusually wide dimensions for a Gothic cathedral, but is surprisingly low.

NAME	Cathedral of Our Lady of Strasbourg (Cathédrale Notre-Dame de Strasbourg)
ADDRESS	rue Mèrciere, Strasbourg, France
CONSTRUCTION HISTORY	1015/1176–1439
	4th–5th century 1st cathedral built
	1015 Present Romanesque cathedral begun; burnt down 1176
	1240 Choir built
	1439 Cathedral completed
COMMISSIONED BY	Bishop Wernher (laid foundation stone of Romanesque cathedral)
ARCHITECTS	Erwin von Steinbach; Ulrich von Ensingen (north steeple); Johann Hültz (spire)
MATERIALS	Pink-gray sandstone
STYLE	Romanesque, High Gothic

During the Reformation many of the cathedral's artefacts were robbed. It was further devastated during the French Revolution, although a remarkable effort at camouflaging secured the safety of the spire. The cathedral was heavily damaged during World War II, and its last repairs were completed only in the 1990s.

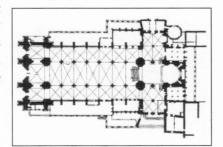

Facing page:
Strasbourg's magnificent Gothic cathedral was said by Goethe to "be composed of a thousand harmonizing details."

Built in pink-gray sandstone, the flying buttresses support the body of the cathedral.

Saintly figures in evocative poses on the exterior.

Holy Savior Cathedral

The cathedral's antecedents go back to the 1st century to a site located on an ancient Roman road, the Via Aurelia. Originally, either a Roman forum or a temple stood here. Christian legend ascribes the first church to being founded by St Maximinus of Aix who is said to have arrived here with Mary Magdalene in a boat, and dedicated the small chapel to the Holy Savior. Other sources testify to the existence of a group of episcopal buildings built over the Roman forum in the 6th century, apparently destroyed by the Saracens. The present cathedral, dedicated to the Virgin Mary, was begun as a parish church on the same site in the 12th century. When a second nave was built, it was dedicated to St Maximinus, and included the oratory of the Holy Savior. With the growing prosperity of Aix when it became the capital of Provence at the end of the 12th century, several religious orders arrived and a spurt in building activity took place, affecting the cathedral as well.

Completed over a period of 500 years, Holy Savior Cathedral expresses a rich mix of architectural styles. Fragments of a Roman wall and the columns of the baptistery remain. The 12th century brought in the Gothic vocabulary with the building of the second nave, the transepts, a new façade, and bell tower. The last bay was constructed in the 15th century, and the statues also installed in this period. Various artists contributed to the decoration of the façade, which included images of the twelve apostles, and creation of the tympanum, the latter unfortunately destroyed during the French Revolution.

NAME	Holy Savior Cathedral (Cathédrale St-Sauveur)
ADDRESS	rue Gaston-de-Saporta, Aix-en-Provence, France
CONSTRUCTION HISTORY	**12th century** Cathedral begun, Roman (Provencal) nave built
	13th century Gothic nave and transepts built
	17th century Nave rebuilt (Baroque); cathedral completed
MATERIALS	Stone, walnut doors
STYLE	Romanesque, Gothic

St-Sauveur is a repository of several masterpieces of art and religious artefacts. Notable amongst these is a set of 17 tapestries originally woven for the Canterbury Cathedral, from where they were taken during the English Civil War, then stolen but repurchased during the French Revolution. In 1977 the first nine of these were again stolen and have not yet been recovered. The *Burning Bush* triptych by Nicolas Froment (15th century) is its most valuable possession. Neo-Gothic decorative pieces belong to the 19th century, including a beautiful stone altar of the Aygosi family, who probably donated a chapel to the cathedral.

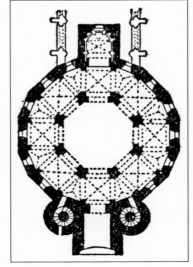

Facing page:
The new Gothic façade of Holy Savior Cathedral features religious images made between the 12th and 15th centuries.

The altar of the Aygosi family.

Triptych of the Burning Bush, by Nicolas Froment.

Laon Cathedral

The first cathedral of Laon was built under the Carolingian rulers, the Frankish founders of France and Germany. The early history of this Roman Catholic cathedral is full of drama. The building was burned in 1112, when the citizens turned in anger against the unpopular Bishop Gaudri, who had annuled their charter and set fire to various shrines and relics. Reconstruction could not begin for several years. Funds were scarce and collected slowly by clergy traveling from town to town soliciting offerings by exhibiting items from the treasuries of other canons. A successful trip to England resulted in collection of enough money to prepare the church in time for its consecration in 1114. The present cathedral is the result of Bishop Gauthier de Montagne's efforts to solicit further funds for a total rebuilding of the cathedral almost 50 years later. The reasons for the reconstruction, however, are unclear.

The effort, which started with the sanctuary and eastern bays of the transept, totally respects the older style of the church, despite the fact that trends had changed. The older choir was demolished and then lengthened so that its final dimensions eventually matched those of the nave. As a result, the transept now cuts the building equally in half. This symmetry is repeated in the design of the rose windows on both the western and the eastern ends and echoes the rose window motif at both ends of the transept façades as well. Laon is distinguished by its two western towers, which rise from the main structure of the building, while the west façade, with its three arched portals, boldly projects outwards. This model was repeatedly followed by many churches of the period.

The nave in four tiers and rebuilt choir match the older parts of the church.

NAME	Cathedral of Our Lady in Laon (Cathédrale Notre-Dame de Laon)
ADDRESS	8 rue du Cloitre, Laon, France
CONSTRUCTION HISTORY	**774–800 CE** 1st church built on site
	1052–1095 2nd church built on site; burnt down 1112
	12th century Cathedral begun and consecrated; rebuilding starts with choir
	13th century Main building complete (1260) with nave, choir, side chapels rebuilt
	14th century South and north façades reconstructed
	1846–1914 restoration
MATERIALS	Stone
STYLE	Gothic

Only five of the seven planned towers flanking the façades are complete, the central one being a lantern-tower illuminating the crossing. The use of white stone further enhances the luminosity of the cathedral, which has been compared to the Paris Notre-Dame. Laon escaped lightly both during the French Revolution and the World Wars.

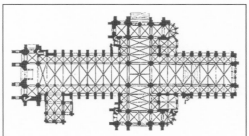

Facing page: Laon Cathedral's front façade is dramatic in its sculptural and architectural detailing.

Meeting of the ribbed vaults and pillar supports at the transept crossing.

Notre-Dame Cathedral

Central to the Roman Catholic faith in France, Notre-Dame Cathedral is perhaps visited even more than the Eiffel Tower. The cathedral was the site of many significant events that assured its place in history: The Crusaders prayed here before surging forth on each campaign; Henry VI of England and Mary Stuart were crowned here; and in 1768 geographers decided that all distances in France would be measured from the cathedral. Further, in 1804 Napoleon crowned himself and Josephine in the church. Here, too, Charles de Gaulle offered thanksgiving after the liberation of Paris in 1944, and it was here that his requiem mass was held. This Gothic wonder stands on the site of a Roman temple to Jupiter, which was replaced by a Christian basilica and then the Romanesque cathedral of Saint Etienne, founded in 528 CE by Childebert I. The present cathedral took almost 200 years to build and was started in 1163 by one of the most remarkable bishops of the time, Maurice de Sully, a wood gatherer's son, who held the position for 36 years.

The cathedral is the work of several architects as can be discerned by differences in style at different heights of the towers and west front. Two sturdy towers dominate the west, between which the elegant spire emerges as a unifying element. This monumental building has a complex buttress system on the exterior that holds up the body of the cathedral, while inside a system of soaring sexpartite vaults rises three stories high. Like Laon, Notre-Dame has three portals, but unlike Laon, it is a dark church, despite the beautiful 13th-century stained glass and jewel-like rose windows.

NAME	Cathedral of Our Lady of Paris (Cathédrale Notre-Dame de Paris)
ADDRESS	6 place du Parvis Notre-Dame, Île de la Cité, 4e Paris, France
CONSTRUCTION HISTORY	528 CE 1st Romanesque cathedral; demolished 1160
	1163 Present cathedral begun and dedicated
	1200–45 West front and towers built
	1345 Cathedral complete
	19th century Major restoration program
COMMISSIONED BY	Childebert I; Bishop Maurice de Sully
ARCHITECTS	Jean Revy (master mason, pinnacles and finials of chapels); Jean de Chelles, Pierre de Montereuil (transept façades); Jean-Baptiste-Antoine Lassus and Eugene Viollet-le-Duc (restoration)
MATERIALS	Stone
STYLE	Gothic; Medieval stained-glass, Romanesque sculpture

Pillaged during the French Revolution and used as a food warehouse, the cathedral was restored in the 19th century under architect Viollet-le-Duc, who also designed the spire. Napoleon's urban planner, Baron Haussmann aided the effort by having the area around the cathedral cleared of houses, revealing traces of Roman buildings. Conservation work is ongoing since the 1990s.

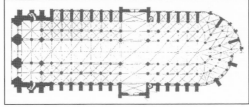

Facing page:
Seen from its eastern end, Notre-Dame integrates form and structure with awesome artistry.

Detail of the sculptural inset in the circular ornamentation all along the nave and eastern end.

Section of a stained-glass window in the choir.

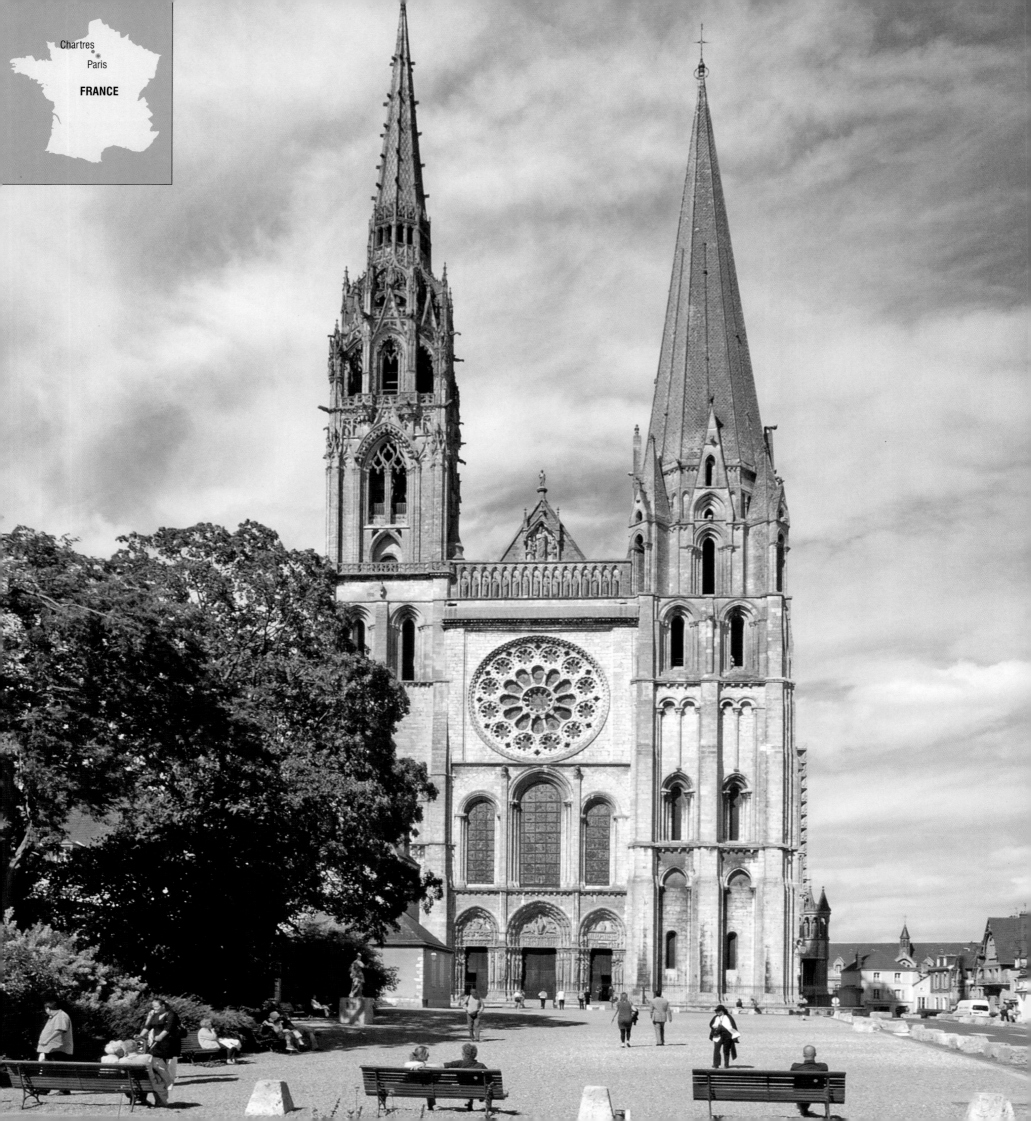

Chartres Cathedral

UNESCO World Heritage Site

Chartres Cathedral has been called the 'triumph' of Gothic art. In France, it is a pilgrimage center of supreme importance, as it houses the tunic said to have been worn by the Virgin Mary when she gave birth to Christ. Received by Charlemagne in 876 CE in Jerusalem as a gift during his Crusade, the tunic was miraculously saved twice, once from the enemy Vikings, and again in 1194 by a great fire that destroyed most of the original church. The relic ensured the future of Chartres as a pilgrimage destination and thus the prosperity of the town. Stories ascribe the fire to an expression of the Virgin's desire for a new and grander church, and indeed Chartres more than lives up to that expectation. Although the architect remains unknown, the cathedral is the largest Gothic creation up to this period, and certainly the most awe inspiring.

Chartres was a pioneer in architectural innovation in many ways. The most important place of pilgrimage in France, it surpassed all its predecessors in grandeur. It uniquely combined all the Gothic elements of earlier churches, borrowed from the militaristic architecture of the time, and yet retained a subtlety of detail. The solidity of the walls creates on overriding impression of strength. Flying buttresses were installed as a support from the start, and internally, the height of the vault—even higher than that of the Notre-Dame in Paris—reinforces this image. However, the brilliance of Chartres lies in the balance between strength and delicacy, enhanced by the rhythmic alternation of piers between round and octagonal, and the size of the windows that seem to make the wall surface dissolve. Chartres' stained-glass windows are legendary—all 186 are originals and the myriad colors of light that percolate through them produce an almost mystical effect.

NAME	Cathedral of Our Lady in Chartres (Cathédrale Notre-Dame de Chartres)
ADDRESS	16 cloitre Notre-Dame, Chartres, France
CONSTRUCTION HISTORY	**1020** 1st cathedral burnt
	1194 Fire by lightning destroys all but the west towers; immediate rebuilding begins
	Early 13th century Main structure complete
	1260 Dedicated
	Early 16th century North spire built
MATERIALS	Bercheres limestone
STYLE	Gothic

Fortunately Chartres was not touched during the French Revolution and so survives in its original form despite necessary restoration work. The friezes and sculptures on its nine portals and elsewhere, the famed rose and other windows, and the ancient stone labyrinth establish its pedigree as one of the greats in cathedral architecture.

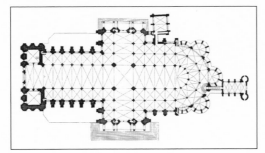

Facing page:
The strength and massiveness of Chartres was influenced by the militaristic castle architecture of the day.

Tympanum of the central bay of the royal portal.

The central part of the stained-glass window in the choir depicts the Marriage at Cana.

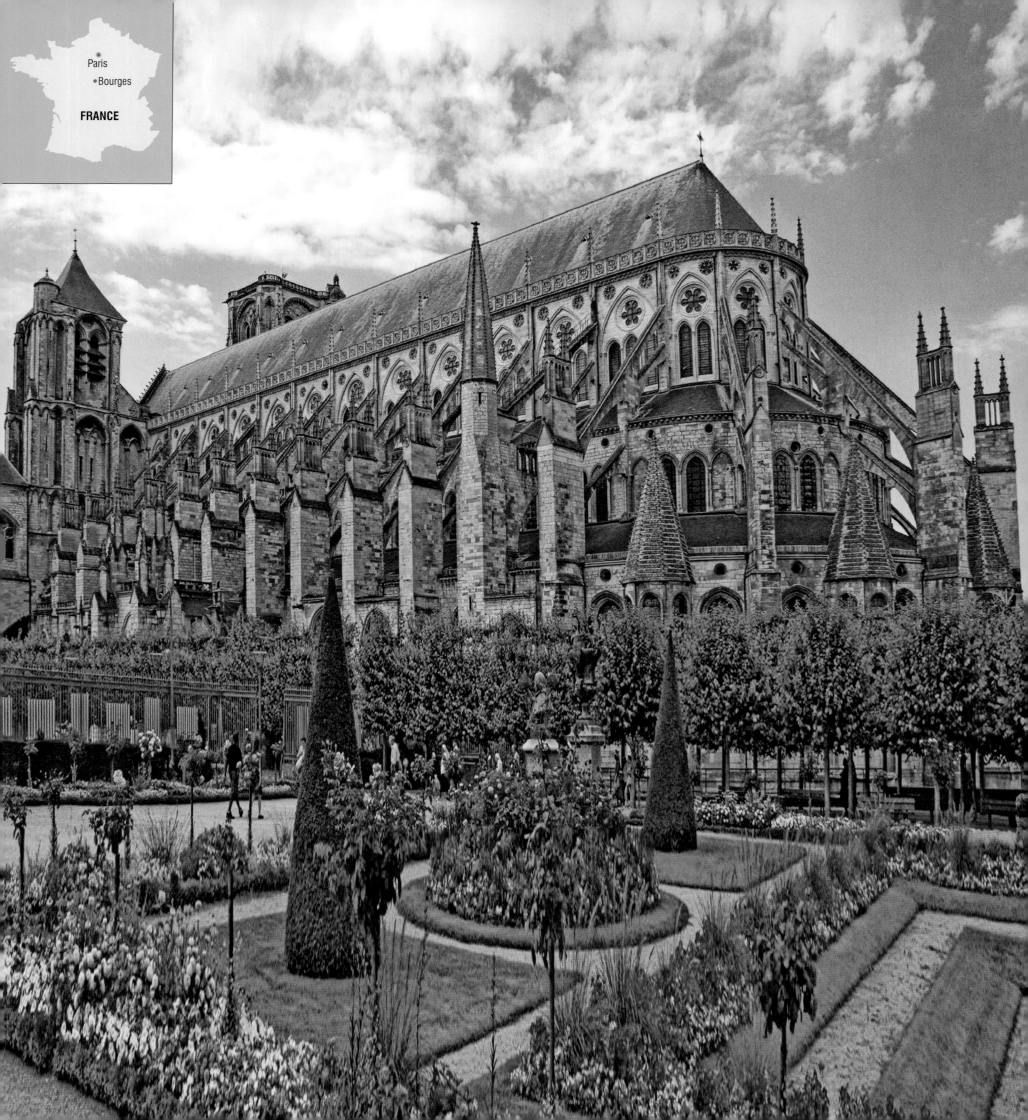

Bourges Cathedral

Eight hundred years before the Roman Catholic cathedral at Bourges was built a 3rd-century Roman city sheltered the first Christian community here. Several monumental crypts are said to have been built on the site, and predictably, the oldest section of the cathedral lies in the lower church, or crypt. The first cathedral, constructed in the 11th century in Romanesque style, was found to be too small. It was rebuilt, funded largely by the Bishop of Bourges, Henri de Sully. Bourges grew in importance as a royal city around this period. The cathedral was the seat of an eminent and powerful bishopric, and the city itself close to the political and architectural center of the region.

The cathedral is unique in that it has no transepts. Other features bear resemblance particularly to Paris's Notre-Dame and Cluny Cathedral. The monumental interior space is its most striking feature. Structurally, this has been made possible by massive piers that support the vaulting. There is an astonishing play of light inside. On the exterior, thick walls and multiple slender flying buttresses lend support to the weight of the nave created inside. The west façade, amongst the broadest of Gothic cathedrals in France, has five portals in all, beautifully carved, one depicting the life of St Stephen to whom the church is dedicated. The stained-glass windows rival those at Chartres in beauty.

NAME	Cathedral of St Stephen (Cathédrale St-Etienne de Bourges)
ADDRESS	place Etienne-Dolet, 18000 Bourges, France
CONSTRUCTION HISTORY	**11th century** 1st cathedral (Romanesque)
	1195 Present cathedral construction begun
	1214–late 13th century Choir; nave; west façade built
	1324 Cathedral dedicated
	1542 North tower rebuilt
COMMISSIONED BY	Archbishop Henri de Sully (initiated the building assisted by the Chapter of canons), followed by Archbishop Guillaume de Dangeon
MATERIALS	Stone
STYLE	High Gothic

Bourges achieved the height of its glory in the mid 15th century. Subsequently, a series of disasters occurred, beginning with cracks in the south tower, followed by collapse of the north tower in 1505. Then came the customary looting during the subsequent Wars of Religion and the French Revolution. Subsequent repairs and additions have maintained its coherence of design however, and the cathedral, surrounded by original cobble-stone pathways and half-timbered houses, is hailed as one of the great monuments of the world.

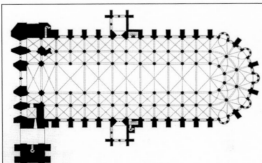

Facing page:
The majesty and grandeur of Bourges Cathedral, seen from the southeast.

The nave is extraordinarily high and wide, creating an impression of monumentality inside.

Most of Bourges's original 25 jewel-like stained-glass windows have survived.

Reims Cathedral

UNESCO World Heritage Site

Reims has long been the coronation church of France. In 496 CE, Clovis, the king of the Franks was anointed here by the Bishop of Reims, and until 1825 it was here that each new French monarch was consecrated. The cathedral was the spiritual heart of the city, which in turn was the urban center of Gaul during Roman times. The earliest church was built by Bishop Nicasius, c. 400 CE. A second church was built (date unknown), and when it burnt down, there was a need to replace it soon in anticipation of the next coronation. The Hundred Years War slowed down the building of the cathedral because of the scarcity of stone, and only when it had been collected by order of Charles VI did construction resume. The story of the victorious Joan of Arc kneeling before Charles VII at his anointment in 1429, holding the standard she had borne from Orleans, marks one of the high points in the church's history.

Reims was begun 15 years after Chartres and relies heavily on the former church as a model, borrowing details from local architectural tradition to further enhance its image as a coronation church. The short choir, inherited from the past, remained, even though the new nave was lengthened. This helped fix attention on the area where the elaborate coronation ceremony was held. Every surface is enriched with either the use of luxuriant natural foliage as a decorative motif, or with figures of saints and martyrs and imagery from the life of Christ. Giant-sized angels circle the exterior, echoing the same motif inside. For the first time in Gothic architecture, a new form of tracery appears in the rose windows.

Detail of statuary above the central portal arch shows Christ the Savior, the Virgin Mary, and others.

NAME	Cathedral of Our Lady of Reims (Cathédrale Notre-Dame de Reims)
ADDRESS	place du Cardinal-Luçon, Reims, France
CONSTRUCTION HISTORY	c. 400 **CE** 1st church exists
	1210–1211 2nd church burnt down; present cathedral construction begins
	13th century Choir, ambulatory, chapels transepts, west façade, nave complete
	15th century Two towers built; cathedral complete 1427; fire destroys roof and spires; restoration work
	17th/19th/20th century Restoration work
ARCHITECTS	Robert de Coucy, Jean d'Orbais, Jean le Loup, Gaucher de Reims, Bernard de Soisson, Viollet-le-Duc
MATERIALS	Chalky limestone
STYLE	High Gothic

The cathedral was damaged in both World Wars; yet it was in Reims that the Germans surrendered unconditionally to the Allies in 1945. The glorious cathedral has been restored by various architects and art historians from the 15th century onwards, including Viollet-le-Duc in the 19th century.

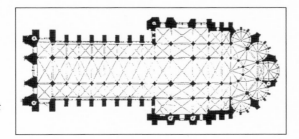

Facing page:
Reims Cathedral's magnificent façade is enriched with countless stone statues.

The central passage of the three-aisled nave surmounted with a great rose window up above.

Amiens Cathedral

UNESCO World Heritage Site

Though not as extravagant as its contemporaries at Reims and Chartres, the monumental cathedral at Amiens is considered the largest of the three great Gothic cathedrals of medieval western Europe. The first record of a bishop of Amiens appears in 346 CE but even before this time there seem to have been two places of worship on the site of the present cathedral. Royal marriages were solemnized in the first one. Its importance grew further when it became a major place of pilgrimage after the head, supposedly that of John the Baptist, was brought by Crusaders from Constantinople in 1206. After the building's destruction by fire, a new cathedral, worthy of this most important relic, was planned, and the foundation stone laid in 1220.

Initially, there was little space for construction, apart from the nave (which comprised the entire area of the older building), because of the proximity of surrounding structures. The foresight in planning the cathedral is therefore remarkable in that it was designed for a future period when, hopefully, land would be available. The various parts of the church have different styles of decoration, but despite this, what emerges is a harmonious whole, which combines different building techniques. The soaring nave has a structural elegance while the interior is lightened by open arcades and large clerestory windows. Externally, a cluster of pointed gables rise above the choir and the gable motif is repeated inside, drawing attention to the High Altar and central space. Particularly arresting is the west front, defined by three recessed arched portals, all elaborately decorated with religious imagery.

NAME	Cathedral of Our Lady of Amiens (Cathédrale Notre-Dame d'Amiens)
ADDRESS	place Notre-Dame, 80021 Amiens, France
CONSTRUCTION HISTORY	**3rd–4th century CE** 1st church
	1137 1st Romanesque cathedral; consecrated 1152
	1218 Cathedral burnt down
	1220–66 Construction of present cathedral, begun with nave, west front; consecrated
	14th–15th century North and south towers
	1850s Restoration work by Viollet-le-Duc
ARCHITECTS	Robert de Luzarches, Thomas de Cormont, Renaud de Cormont
MATERIALS	Stone
STYLE	High Gothic

Several times through history the cathedral has suffered damage but escaped lightly during the two world wars, except for a fire which destroyed the beautiful collection of stained glass stored for safe keeping in the artists' studio. Since the end of the 20th century laser cleaning techniques have been used revealing the superb details of the structure.

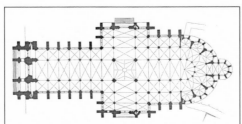

Facing page:
Amiens Cathedral was originally painted in multiple colors which highlighted its sculptural richness.

The façade of Amiens is sculpted with figures of kings and saints.

Although vast, the interior is surprisingly bright, retaining much of the original stained glass.

FRANCE

Paris

Narbonne

Narbonne Cathedral

The Roman Catholic cathedral of Narbonne in southern France, seat of the archbishop, was once an important port city, rivaling Marseilles. Towering above the small town, the 13th-century cathedral appears complete at first glance, but in fact was never finished after the choir and transept were built. Further building would have meant knocking down the Roman defensive walls nearby, and this was considered premature because of a possible English invasion. Wars and epidemics also halted further construction, but despite its incomplete status, this is often referred to as the only Gothic cathedral of the Mediterranean region that can rival some of the best in northern France. The cathedral stands next door to the Palace of the Archbishops of Narbonne, to which it is connected through the cloisters. Together, the buildings form an interesting architectural ensemble.

Narbonne's strong point is its vaulted choir, which echoes the bold imagery of France's northern cathedrals. It rises 130 ft (39 m) high and contains the High Altar in marble and gilded bronze, gifted by Cardinal de Bonzo, archbishop from 1673–1703. At each end of the transept are the late 15th-century towers, the left containing the treasures of the cathedral, which include some exquisite pieces of Flemish tapestry. Tombs, statues, manuscripts, and other religious objects can also be seen in the chapels around the apse.

NAME	St Just and St Pasteur Cathedral
ADDRESS	place de l'Hôtel-de-Ville, Narbonne, France
CONSTRUCTION HISTORY	1272 Construction begun; mostly complete 1340 **1480** Towers built
ARCHITECTS	Eugene Emmanuel Viollet-le-Duc. Dominique and Jacques de Fauran, Jean Deschamps
MATERIALS	Stone
STYLE	Gothic

Narbonne had its own diocese until it was merged with the Diocese of Carcassone to be renamed the Diocese of Carcassone and Narbonne in 2006. In 2000 for the first time, the great reredos behind the altar was unveiled, revealing sculptured panels of Jesus's triumphal entry into Jerusalem, and graphic depictions of Paradise and Purgatory.

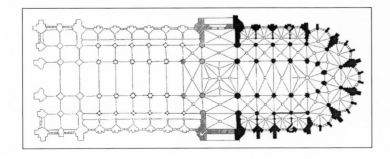

Facing page:
Narbonne Cathedral rises out of the mass of surrounding buildings including the Palace of Archbishops.

The old Roman wall around the cathedral.

The state of disrepair in certain sections is evidence of the incomplete nature of the cathedral.

Albi Cathedral

Albi Cathedral was built as a fortress during the early 13th-century Albigensian Crusade. This 20-year long military campaign was instigated by the Pope to reign in the breakaway Cathars who lived in large numbers in and around Albi. Located at a strategic point above the river Tarn, the Gothic cathedral served a functional purpose and made a political statement about the authority of the Church. It was declared a cathedral by the Bishop of Albi, who was also Inquisitor of the region during the campaign. As bishop he seized the opportunity to build a new church, which was the fourth to be built here. The earlier structures had been destroyed either by fire or by the wars of the heretics. The cathedral takes its name from St Cecilia, patron saint of musicians and church music, who died singing.

Formidable in appearance, solid buttresses at the west entrance declare the militaristic intention of the cathedral. Buttresses also line the aisleless interior. Albi is one of the great examples of Romanesque churches in the south of France. Its exaggerated, elongated vertical space inside continues over the entire vaulted length of the church, including the choir. It is elaborately decorated with filigree work, statues and frescoes, and presents a surprising contrast to the stark exterior. Frescoes on the ceiling lay claim to be the oldest collection of Italian Renaissance paintings in France. Most noteworthy is the mural of *The Last Judgment*, somewhat terrifying in its portrayal of Hell. Part of it was destroyed to provide access to a chapel at the base of the bell tower. Another highlight is the rood-screen of exquisitely carved and painted statues.

NAME	Cathedral of St Cecilia
ADDRESS	Place du Vigan, Albi, Midi-Pyrenees, France
CONSTRUCTION HISTORY	**4th century** 1st church; destroyed by fire in 666 CE
	920 CE 2nd church
	1282 Romanesque stone cathedral begun
	14th–late 15 century Choir (1330); belfry (1355-66); 1480 consecrated; octagonal upper part of tower, rood-screen (1485-c.1490s)
COMMISSIONED BY	Bernard de Castanet, Bishop of Albi (Patron)
MATERIALS	Brick, stone gargoyles
STYLE	Romanesque, southern Gothic

Albi Cathedral is one of the world's most important brick buildings. Later additions include the 16th-century bell tower over the entrance and frescoes of the same period in the vault. The Treasury contains liturgical objects dating up to the 19th century.

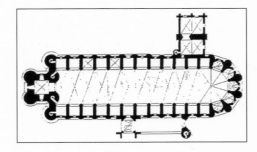

Facing page:
Albi Cathedral is made of solid brick with none of the delicate stonework of its Gothic contemporaries.

Unlike the forbidding exterior, the inside of the cathedral is enriched by expressive statues, sculpture, and paintings.

The vault frescoes are the largest work of Italian Renaissance painting found anywhere in France.

Aachen Cathedral

Aachen Cathedral's core is the small Palatine Chapel that was built by Charlemagne in the 8th century. Part of a palace complex, it was the coronation church for 30 German kings over a period of 600 years. Charlemagne was buried in the cathedral and two accounts of the opening of his vault record his unique status. The first, written around 1026, describes the discovery of his incorruptible body in a sitting position holding a scepter. The second time round, the vault was opened by Emperor Frederick Barbarossa, who then placed his remains in a sarcophagus—later transfered to a casket of silver and gold.

Charlemagne had been impressed with the sacred sites of Ravenna's St Vitale and the Hagia Sophia of Constantinople and based his magnificent Palatine Chapel on them. It was octagonal in plan and opulently decorated with gilded mosaics in the Byzantine mode. The Shrine of St Mary, to whom the cathedral is dedicated, houses four precious pieces of clothing, belonging separately to the Blessed Virgin, the Infant Jesus, John the Baptist, and to Christ's loin cloth worn on the Cross. The cathedral contains other rare exhibits, such as the Cross of Lothair and the Persephone sarcophagus, making it one of the most precious repositories of sacred relics in northern Europe. Along with the Gothic choir, the west steeple, the portal, and other chapels were made at later dates, resulting in the present edifice. The golden Shrine of Charlemagne also rests in the choir, although his remains were further divided into two separate reliquaries in the mid-14th century.

NAME	Aachen Cathedral (Pfalzkapelle, Kaiserdom, Palatine Chapel, Aachener Dom)
ADDRESS	Klosterplatz 2, 52062 Aachen, Germany
CONSTRUCTION HISTORY	**786–805 CE** Palatine Chapel built and consecrated 805 CE
	13th century Shrines of St Mary and Charlemagne built
	15th century Choir, Glass Chapel consecrated; smaller chapels added
	17th century West portal built
COMMISSIONED BY	Charles the Great (Charlemagne)
ARCHITECT	Odo of Metz
MATERIALS	Stone
STYLE	Carolingian, Byzantine, Gothic

During the French Revolution most of the decorative columns of the gallery, brought from Rome and Ravenna, were stolen but have since been returned. World War II bombings destroyed the original windows, which have also been replaced.

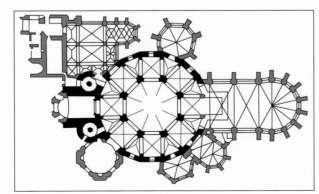

Facing page: Aachen Cathedral has been described as a "masterpiece of Carolingian architecture".

Studded with precious stones, the pulpit is a shining example of Gothic goldwork.

The vaulted cupola is gilded and painted with the figure of Christ surrounded by the 24 Ancients of the Apocalypse.

Augsburg Cathedral

The town of Augsburg in Bavaria was founded by Emperor Tiberius in 15 BCE and is the gateway to the south of Germany. Recorded evidence of the cathedral's history mentions 823 CE as the earliest date. Foundations beneath the building, however, go back to the 4th century though it is uncertain whether they were part of a church. It is believed that St Sintpert (*c.* 810 CE), a relative of Charlemagne, renovated many churches and monasteries that had been destroyed in the wars between the Franks and Bavarians. Augsburg Cathedral is said to have been built by him in honor of the Most Blessed Virgin. Successive bishops actively propagated the faith through sustained efforts at restoration and building of collegiate churches. Augsburg attained its greatest splendor in the 10th century. However, ongoing conflict between the church and state affected its growth, until Bishop Hartmann in the 13th century bequeathed to the church his paternal inheritance, thus ensuring peace. The cathedral was rebuilt in the 15th century, and as the city of Augsburg prospered, so too did its cathedral.

First begun in the Roman style, the cathedral was remodeled around 1331 as a Gothic church and the lofty east choir with its radiating chapels was added. In the 15th–16th centuries, the towers were increased in height. The cathedral has been rebuilt several times, during which many art treasures have been lost, resulting in an interior that, while not stylistically harmonious, is interesting in the details. The last significant rebuilding in 1863 followed the Neo-Gothic style. The south clerestory contains the oldest stained-glass windows in Germany from the 11th–12th centuries, depicting the prophets Moses, David, and others. Paintings by Hans Holbein the Elder (1493) on the nave pillars are other highlights of the decorative interior.

Southern aisles of the nave, looking east.

NAME	High Cathedral of the Virgin Mary
ADDRESS	Augsburg, Bavaria, Germany
CONSTRUCTION HISTORY	*c.* **9th century** 1st cathedral building
	1043–1065 Romanesque structure of present building
	1331–1431 Remodeling in Gothic of choir, and other additions
	1480 Towers complete
COMMISSIONED BY	Bishop Heinrich II
MATERIALS	Red brick, bronze doors
STYLE	Romanesque, Gothic, Baroque Lady Chapel

Part of the cathedral was damaged during World War II but restored in 1987–88. A late addition to the cathedral's artistic treasures includes the modern bronze doors by Max Faller, installed in 2000 to replace the Romanesque bronze doors of 1065.

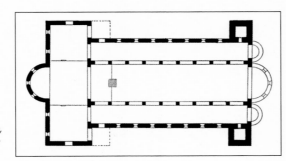

Facing page:
Augsburg Cathedral is a fine blend of the Romanesque style, here seen in the tower, and the Gothic, seen in the east choir.

Romanesque eastern crypt.

GERMANY

Berlin

Mainz

Mainz Cathedral

Considered one of the trinity of 'Emperor's Cathedrals' in Germany along with Speyer and Worms, Mainz Cathedral was where several German monarchs were crowned between the 11th and 13th centuries. Before then the town had already become a flourishing urban center, and the influential 10th-century prince bishop, Willigis, dreamed of it as the second Rome, boasting a church comparable to St Peter's. Thus not only was it commissioned with St Peter's in mind, it also had to accommodate the functions of two churches—the old St John's (then St Salvator), which had been consecrated in 911 CE as the seat of the Archbishop of Mainz, and St Albans, the largest church in the area. In 1188 the Holy Roman Emperor Frederick Barbarossa launched the Third Crusade from here. The Roman Catholic cathedral of today is the result of continual rebuilding and restoration over 1000 years.

Since the final form took centuries to emerge, various architectural influences are apparent. Primarily a Romanesque structure, it had a triple nave cross pattern, two choirs, several side chapels, and two transepts. Six towers soared upwards, but there was no vault to begin with. Henry IV took a keen interest in reconstruction after the damage caused by two major fires, and modeled much of the building on Speyer Cathedral, another pet project of his. However, funds dried up with his death, and work came to a halt. Almost 100 years later, the ceiling was replaced by a ribbed vault. From the 12th until the 19th century—when Napoleon's passionate interest in architecture did much to preserve historic legacies—changes and additions were continuous, transforming the existing forms in either Gothic or Baroque style.

An aura of sobriety and serenity fills the cloisters.

NAME	St Martin's Cathedral (Mainzer Dom, Martinsdom, Der Hohe Dom zu Mainz)
ADDRESS	Domstrasse 3, Mainz, Germany
CONSTRUCTION HISTORY	**10th–11th century** Present cathedral built
	1110–37 Gotthard Chapel built
	13th–15th century Ribbed vault, Gothic chapels, eastern and western towers completed; Nassauer Chapel built (1418)
	1769 Baroque roofs for western towers
COMMISSIONED BY	Archbishop Willigis; Henry IV (reconstruction of east side with chancel, dome, crypt, apse, etc)
ARCHITECTS	Madern Gerthener (Nassauer Chapel); Franz Ignza Michael Neumann (western tower roofs)
MATERIALS	Sandstone, limestone, red marble flooring
STYLE	Romanesque, Gothic, Baroque

At the end of World War I, contemporary materials—concrete and steel—were used to reinforce both the foundations and the towers. A new red marble floor was installed, which soon, however, lost its color. Whatever little was destroyed during World War II was restored as authentically as possible, and in 1975 the cathedral celebrated its 1000-year anniversary.

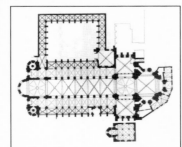

Facing page:
Mainz Cathedral is primarily Romanesque in style, with later additions in Gothic or Baroque.

Almost a millennium of Christian art can be seen inside the church, starting from the basement, through its various chapels and altars.

GERMANY

Berlin

Speyer

Speyer Cathedral

Speyer Cathedral in the Roman Catholic archdiocese of Bamberg is dedicated to St Mary, patron saint of Speyer, and to St Stephen. As the burial place for Habsburg rulers, it was recognized as a symbol of imperial power. Commissioned by Conrad II on the site of a former basilica, the cathedral was built in two distinct phases, known as Speyer I and Speyer II. The second phase, carried out by Conrad's grandson, Henry IV, involved an ambitious reconstruction, which was also a political affirmation of the secular and spiritual power of the emperor, undermining the religious supremacy of the papacy. It resulted in Henry's excommunication, a decision that was, however, revoked five years after the emperor's death. Damaged by a great town fire in 1689, the cathedral was restored to its original state almost 100 years later.

A turning point in European architecture, the cathedral introduced elements that influenced the development of the Romanesque style. Thus, when Henry IV enlarged the eastern sections, a cross vault replaced the earlier wooden ceiling, raising the height of the nave and putting in place a double-bay system, a feature copied in many monuments along the Rhine. Another innovation was the blind arcaded gallery circling the apse both inside and outside. When completed, Speyer was one of the largest buildings of its time. Its marvelous four towers with conical roofs in oxidized copper frame the nave and domes at both ends, and with the polychrome *Westwerk*, make a wonderful composition.

NAME	Imperial Cathedral Basilica of the Assumption and St Stephen (Kaiserdom zu Speyer)
ADDRESS	Alstadt, Speyer, Rhineland-Palatinate, Germany
CONSTRUCTION HISTORY	**1030–1061** Speyer I built; consecrated **1090–1106** Speyer II built **1689** Nave burnt down, restored 1778 **Mid 19th century** interior painted, west front rebuilt
COMMISSIONED BY	Conrad II
ARCHITECTS	Franz Ignaz M Neumann (18th century); Heinrich Hübsch (*Westwork* 19th century)
MATERIALS	Red sandstone
STYLE	Romanesque, Gothic, Baroque

Ludwig I had ordered the entire interior painted in the mid-19th century. During restoration in the 1950s, the color was removed to reveal the magnificent architectural detailing. Most of the buildings originally surrounding the cathedral were destroyed during the French Revolution. Only the outline of the cloister remains as a pavement. A Hall of Antiques has now become a memorial to those killed in the two World Wars, and current efforts at restoration are expected to continue until 2015.

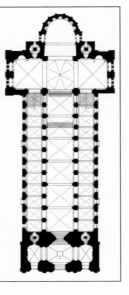

Facing page:
The west front of Speyer Cathedral in alternating color bands is both austere and elegantly decorative.

At the chevet end, the apse wall is animated by an arcaded gallery resting on long, slender colonettes.

The large bowl known as Domnapf, which each bishop on his election had to fill with wine.

GERMANY

Berlin

Worms

Worms Cathedral

Two earlier buildings preceded the present, unique Romanesque cathedral at Worms—the first of which was built under Bishop Berthulf in the 7th century, and the second, 400 years later, under Bishop Burchard. Though a small town on the Rhine River, Worms is associated with significant events in its history and particularly the history of the cathedral. The papal election of Leo IX took place here in the 11th century, as well as the Concordat of Worms that terminated the first phase of the struggle between the Pope and the Holy Roman Emperors. In 1521 the Diet of Worms condemned Martin Luther for refusing to recant his religious beliefs, and in 1526 the first complete edition of the New Testament in English was secretly printed here. The town existed before Roman times, when it is believed to have been captured and fortified into a garrison, with temples upon whose remains the cathedral was built.

The current structure, built through the efforts of Bishop Conrad II, retains the plan of its predecessor. The oldest part is the east choir, with a very local style of rounded walls on the inside. Animal figures decorate the arcades, particularly lions, perhaps to ward off the devil. The west choir is a counterpoint to the east, a polygonal apse extending beyond the two towers that abut it. Decorative rose windows and rich moldings ornament it. The east choir is flanked by stair turrets on either side, a characteristic feature of Romanesque German architecture. At the crossing, surmounted by an octagonal tower, is a Baroque extravaganza—the High Altar of gilded wood and marble. The Gothic touch is evident in the font located in the Chapel of St Nicholas off the south aisle and the five tympana in the north aisle.

Much of the original Romanesque architecture and sculpture have been preserved in the cathedral.

NAME	Church of St Peter (Wormser Dom, Dom St Peter)
ADDRESS	Lutherring 9, Worms, Germany
CONSTRUCTION HISTORY	*c.* **614 CE** 1st cathedral
	11th century 2nd cathedral
	1125–81 Present cathedral built (east end, nave, chancel, west end); consecrated 1181
COMMISSIONED BY	Bishop Berthulf, Bishop Conrad II
MATERIALS	Red sandstone
STYLE	High Romanesque

Bombed heavily during World War II, large areas of the city center were destroyed. Apart from other damage, the cathedral lost its original windows. These were, however, replaced gradually until 1995. As principal church and one of the three Roman imperial cathedrals on the northern Upper Rhine, the cathedral stands like a castle fortress, dignified and simple, even though most of it today is the result of restoration and rebuilding over centuries.

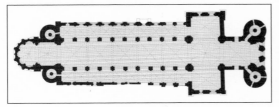

Facing page:
The Church of St Peter at Worms is one of the three great imperial cathedrals on the Upper Rhine, along with those of Speyer and Mainz.

Detail of a line-up of statues of saints, kings, the apostles, and divine figures.

GERMANY
Berlin
Cologne

Cologne Cathedral

Acclaimed as the largest Gothic church in northern Europe, Cologne Cathedral took over 600 years to build. It is thought that the earliest structures on the site were grain stores, followed by a Roman temple. The first, square house of prayer dates to the 4th century, and was commissioned by the first bishop of Cologne, Maternus. The ruins of a baptistery and font can still be seen in the present cathedral though the baptistery was demolished when the 'Old Cathedral' was built in the 9th century. Plans to enlarge it were prepared when it became too small and 'old-fashioned'. Work began after much of it was destroyed by fire. The scale was to be appropriate for housing the precious relics of the Three Magi, earlier brought from Milan by the emperor Fredrick Barbarossa. They gave the city prime status on the pilgrimage map.

A monument to German Catholicism, the cathedral was envisioned as the architectural culmination of all ecclesiastical buildings in Germany. It was the seat of the powerful archbishop Konrad von Hochstaden, who insisted that it reflect a classicism of utmost elegance and purity, modeled on the French Gothic cathedral of Amiens. The interior has double side aisles, permitting the two towers to sit squarely from the ground upwards, and thus allow for a monumental front façade. After an initial spurt in building followed by a long gap, building resumed in the 19th century with the discovery of the cathedral's plans and with the Romantics' enthusiasm for the Middle Ages. More modern methods of construction and state funding were provided, largely to gain favor with Roman Catholic subjects.

Detail of statuary at the Gothic southern transept façade.

NAME	Cologne Cathedral (Kölner dom)
ADDRESS	Domkloster 4, Cologne, North Rhine-Westphalia, Germany
CONSTRUCTION HISTORY	*c.* **4th century CE** 1st church
	818 CE 2nd church (Old Cathedral)
	818 Old cathedral damaged by fire; construction of present cathedral begins
	1824 Towers built
	1880 Cathedral completed and consecrated
ARCHITECTS	Gerhard, Arnold, Johannes
MATERIALS	Stone
STYLE	Gothic, Neo-Gothic

The cathedral's completion in 1880 was celebrated as a national event, attended by Emperor Wilhelm I. Though bombed several times during World War II, it did not collapse, its twin spires in fact acting as navigational guides for the Allied forces. (Evidently the church was also used as a rifle range by American forces.) A process of renovation continues, the most recent addition being a stained-glass window in the south transept.

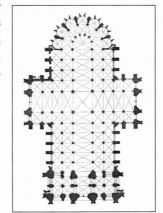

Facing page:
Cologne's most famous landmark is its cathedral, described by UNESCO as "an exceptional work of human creative genius."

Altarpiece of the Three Kings (Magi) at the birth of Christ.

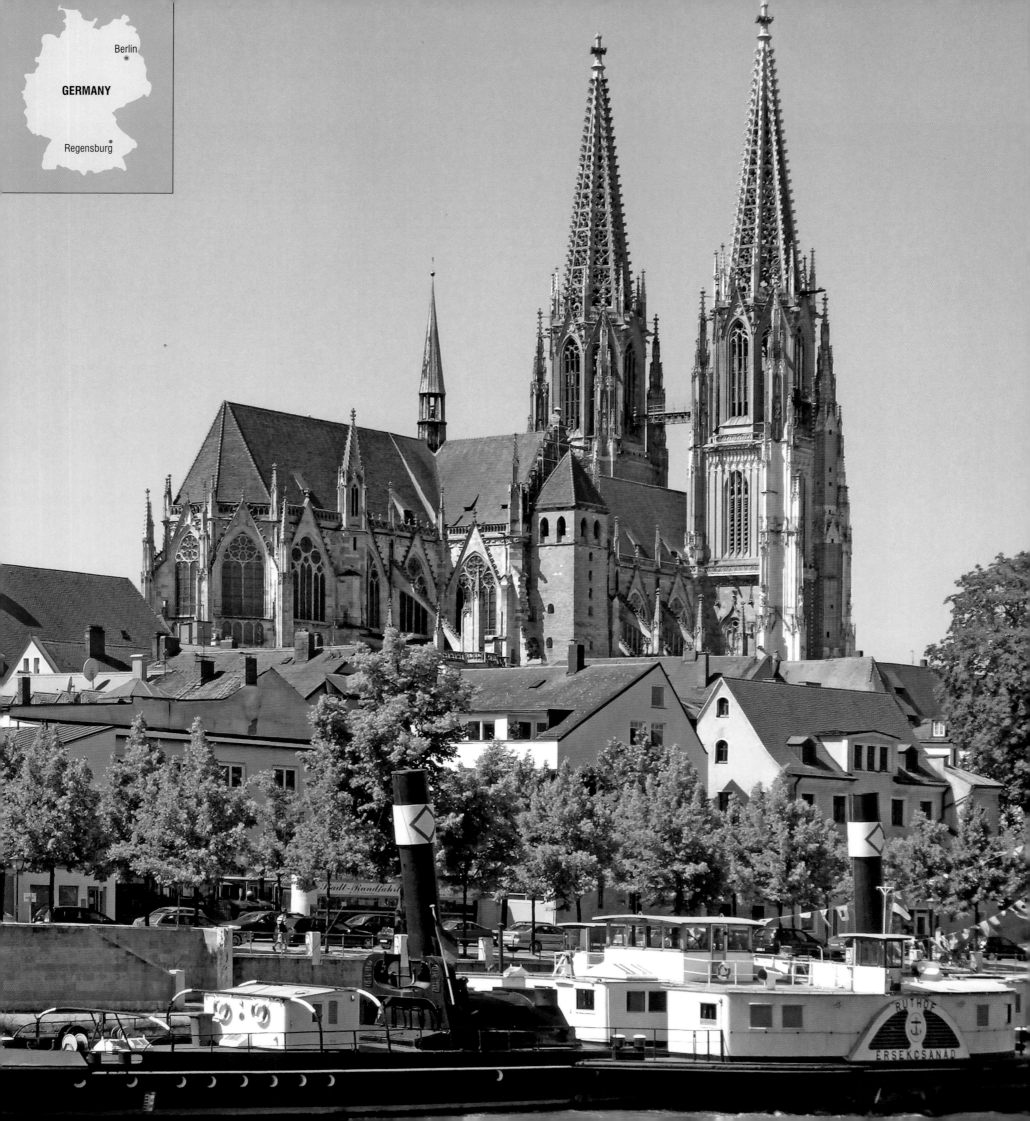

GERMANY

Berlin

Regensburg

Regensburg Cathedral

Dedicated to St Peter, Regensburg Cathedral dates back to the early 8th century when the diocese of Regensburg was established by St Boniface. Nearly 100 images of St Peter adorn the exterior and interior. Several churches stood on this site, the first of which was replaced in the 11th century; the 12th century saw another replacement, followed by the present building, which was begun in the mid-13th century. The church was gradually enlarged to encompass all the essential architectural features of a cathedral and finally considered complete in the mid-19th century. During excavations, the ruins of what is possibly a Roman atrium were discovered in the south arcade. The present cathedral's predecessors followed the style of the period and so, although Gothic is the predominant vocabulary evident now, the church bears traces of its Carolingian, Romanesque, and Baroque history.

The twin towers of the cathedral are visible from all over the city, but are nowhere more impressive than when you approach the city from the Danube, skirting the west. On drawing near, you notice the three west portals, each leading to an aisle that culminates in an altar, the central one being the High Altar. Additional altars are housed in niches in the side aisles. Arches, sculptures, and canopies ornament the west front, while inside, the *Smiling Angel* is one of the most evocative pieces of statuary. The only chapel— called the Sailer Chapel—was built by King Ludwig I in 1837 in honor of his tutor. Like most German Gothic cathedrals, St Peter's abandons the transept and ambulatory, resulting in a compact floor plan. The Gothic-style vault was a 19th-century addition ordered by Ludwig I to replace the 17th-century Baroque dome.

Gothic elements in stone stand out against the red sloped roof above the nave.

NAME	Cathedral of St Peter (Regensburger Dom, Dom St Peter)
ADDRESS	Domplatz 1, 93047 Regensburg, Bavaria, Germany
CONSTRUCTION HISTORY	1260–1520
	c. **700 CE** 1st cathedral
	c. **8th/9th century** Rebuilt; extended 11th century
	1260 Present cathedral begun
	14th–17th century South and north towers, west façade built; nave roofed; cloisters, dome over crossing built
	19th century Dome replaced with ribbed vault; transept gable and spire built
CONSECRATED	1276 (1st altar); 1320 (altars at east end)
MATERIALS	Stone
STYLE	Gothic (earlier Romanesque, Baroque)

The last century saw several notable additions, including a burial crypt for bishops. In 2004 the Sailer Chapel was dedicated as a place for private prayer and services. In 2008 white stone blocks from the Czech Republic were commissioned to replace the weathered green limestone used in earlier restoration efforts.

Facing page:
The great Gothic twin spires of Regensburg Cathedral soar above the low-lying roofscape in the heart of the Old Town.

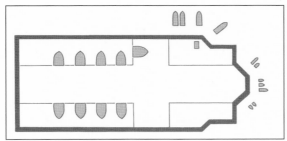

An illuminated painting of Mother and Child encased in an arched niche.

EGO SUM VIA VERITAS ET VITA

Budapest

HUNGARY

St Stephen's Basilica

UNESCO World Heritage Site

This enormous Roman Catholic cathedral, which can accommodate 8500 people, was completed within 50 years despite a major set-back when the dome collapsed. The structural disaster necessitated rebuilding from the ground upwards again. The basilica is dedicated to St Stephen, Hungary's first king, who converted nomadic Hungarian tribes to Christianity, thus establishing a strong link between the eastern European states and those to the west. Luckily nobody died when the dome fell and it is rumored that at the cathedral's consecration the emperor Francis Joseph kept looking upwards fearful of a similar mishap. Despite the original plans being ready in 1845, construction could only begin 10 years later because of the Hungarian Revolution and War of Independence of 1848/49 against Austrian Habsburg rule.

Three architects oversaw the building of the basilica. The first, József Hild, who had designed it but did not live to see it finished; the second, Miklos Ybl, who replaced Hild, and drew up new plans in a Neo-Renaissance style when the dome collapsed, but also died before the work could be completed; and Jozsef Krauser, who finally saw it through to its end, when it was consecrated by the emperor. The difference in styles under the first two architects is clearly visible, especially in the entrance façade. Built on the Greek cruciform plan, the vast dome is upheld by four pillars. A fresco of God the Father dominates the center of the cupola inside. A precious treasure of the cathedral is the relic of St Stephen in the form of his mummified right fist, which is preserved in an ornate glass cabinet in a chapel. Statues of the apostles decorate the outside walls, while the High Altar is adorned with a statue of St Stephen being crowned by the angel Gabriel.

NAME	St Stephen's Basilica (Szent István-bazilika)
ADDRESS	V Szent István tér 33, Pest, Budapest, Hungary
CONSTRUCTION HISTORY	**1855–1905** Cathedral built and consecrated
	1868 Dome collapsed
ARCHITECTS	József Hild, Miklos Ybl, József Krauser
MATERIALS	Stone, Carrara marble (High Altar)
STYLE	Neo-Classical, Neo-Renaissance

Because of its closeness to the Danube River, the basilica had to have very deep foundations and therefore a huge underground cellar. Here, fortunately, the art treasures and documents of the church were kept and survived the bombings during World War II even though the building itself suffered heavy damages. Reconstruction work only started in the 1980s and the basilica is now restored to its original glory.

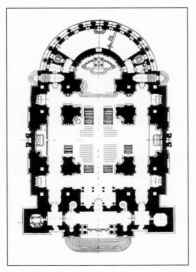

Facing page:
Overlooking St Stephen's Square is Budapest's huge Neo-Classical basilica.

In this magnificent display of frescoes inside the cupola God the Father is the central figure.

The entrance door is heavily carved with portraits of saints and other prime figures related to the history of the cathedral.

Christ Church Cathedral

The history of the cathedral is linked with its changing governance. It was under the Danish Viking king, Sitric Silkenbeard, that the first church was built for the Diocese of Dublin, which at that time was answerable to Canterbury. Almost a century later it was incorporated into the Church of Ireland. The second Archbishop of Dublin, Laurence O'Toole (12th century) reformed the constitution of the cathedral, establishing it as an Augustine Priory along European canonical lines. He was later canonized. The Anglo-Norman capture of the city, the Reformation of the 16th century, and subsequent events all brought about drastic changes in administration. The church's crypt was even used as a market and a pub during the 16th and 17th centuries. The disestablishment of the Church of Ireland in 1871 cut into its endowments. Members of the laity now joined hands with the clergy in its governance. Today it functions as the mother church for the United Dioceses of Dublin and Glendalough.

Medieval in appearance, the church went through a complete rebuilding under Anglo-Norman domination. The crypt, several chapels, the choir, and transepts were all made anew. A chapel to St Laurence O'Toole was added in the 1200s. Because of its shaky foundations (on peat) sections of the nave sank in 1562 bringing down the south wall and arched stone roof. A simple process of leveling and new flooring was conducted. However, not until Victorian times was extensive renovation carried out which, in certain areas makes it difficult to distinguish what is originally medieval. Even the tomb of Strongbow, the Norman Welsh lord who came to Ireland and funded a major part of the building, appears to be a substitute structure. The church's 19 bells range from the 11th to end 20th century.

Ruins of the Chapter House of the priory at the cathedral.

NAME	Cathedral of the Holy Trinity
ADDRESS	Christ Church P and Winetavern St, Dublin 8, Ireland
CONSTRUCTION HISTORY	**1038** 1st wooden church on site
	1170s Church expanded and rebuilt in stone; crypt constructed
	1230s Nave almost complete
	1358 Choir extended
	1870s Restoration resulting in present cathedral
COMMISSIONED BY	King Sitric Silkenbeard
ARCHITECT	George Edmund Street (19th century restoration)
MATERIALS	Stone
STYLE	Norman, Romanesque, Gothic

The cathedral's choir traces its origins to the 15th century and plays an important role in the city's cultural life. Restoration is ongoing with the latest works being carried out in the 1980s–90s on the roof, stonework, and crypt, and with the lighting and heating systems being updated to state of the art technology.

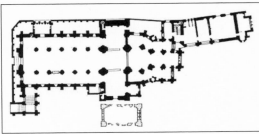

Facing page:
Though outwardly medieval in appearance the church was extensively restored in Victorian times.

The central nave looking towards the High Altar.

St Patrick's Cathedral

St Patrick's is one of four Celtic parish churches in Dublin. Dedicated to St Patrick, who brought Christianity to Dublin, it is not the seat of a bishop, but is regarded as the National Cathedral for all of Ireland, which now includes 28 chapters. Little remains of the first church to have been built on this site except for the baptistery. The present cathedral was begun under the Anglo-Norman bishop John Comyn. Following the Reformation the church fell into disrepair. Over the centuries it was used variously as a court house, a school. a stables, and in 1666 as a refuge for fleeing Huguenots from France. Briefly reverting to its Roman Catholic status in the late 1600s when it was partly restored, it is today the largest Protestant cathedral in a predominantly Roman Catholic country.

Standing on peaty soil the cathedral has always had a problem with seepage of water because of which it does not have a crypt. A prominent Dean of the cathedral in the early part of the 1800s was the famous writer Jonathan Swift, under whom it became central to the life of the community but deteriorated in its physical form. Although its origins go back to early Norman times, the overarching style of the building is Gothic, owing to major rebuilding which took place in the late 1800s. The wealthy Guinness family of Irish brewery fame initiated and paid for the repairs and restoration work. Inside, decorative ironwork and woodwork adorn the choir area, and above the stalls hang the helmets, swords, and banners of Knights of the Order of St Patrick.

NAME	The National Cathedral and Collegiate Church of St Patrick (Arg-Eaglais Naomh Pádraig)
ADDRESS	21-50 Patrick's Close, Dublin 8, Ireland
CONSTRUCTION HISTORY	**5th century–c. 1191** 1st wooden church on site; raised to cathedral status 1191
	c. 1190s–1270 Present cathedral built; Lady Chapel added; cathedral considered complete
	1362–70 Minot's Tower and west nave rebuilt following a fire
	1668–80 Roof rebuilt; choir remodeled
	1769 Spire added
	1870 Major rebuilding
COMMISSIONED BY	King Henry III (reconstruction in 12
STYLE	Norman, Gothic

Until the mid 20th century only Roman Catholics were allowed inside. Recently, in 2006, Afghan refugees took asylum here and had to be persuaded to leave.

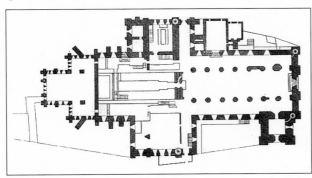

Facing page:
St Patrick's Cathedral is central to the life of the local community.

The statue of Benjamin Guinness, a major benefactor of the cathedral.

Section of the mosaic-tiled floor inside.

IRELAND

Dublin

St Mary's Pro-Cathedral

St Mary's Pro-Cathedral is the main Roman Catholic church in Dublin. However, until the official status of cathedral, accorded to Christ Church by the Pope in the 12th century is not revoked, the latter church, even though it broke away from Roman Catholicism after the Reformation, is still seen as the primary official Dublin cathedral. St Mary's origins are tied to the 12th-century Benedictine Abbey of St Mary's. After the abbey lands were confiscated in the 16th century and all connections with the Pope were to be broken, the land was subdivided and eventually, by an Act of Parliament in 1697, a plot was allotted for the parish of St Mary. The first pastor managed to save enough money to build the first St Mary's Chapel on Liffey Street. Almost a century later, the Dominican archbishop of Dublin requested papal permission for a larger church to be made. Political turmoil delayed the project until finally plans and a model were prepared, and construction began.

The form, copied from the Temple of Theseus in Athena, is in the Greek Revival style. The inclusion of a dome however, invited mixed reactions. Some even called it "a beautiful deformity". From 1821 onwards, when the shell of the dome was complete, the work proceeded in fits and starts. Income from the vaults of the church contributed greatly to its costs. Embellishments and additions continued during the terms of successive archbishops. By the 19th century, the highly ornate style of Victorian decoration had been adopted. Frescoes, statuary, traceries, gilt lettering were all profusely used. Two beautiful altars to Our Lady and the Sacred Heart were added in 1908. The 1900s have seen a new St Kevin's Chapel and also a new altar to St Laurence O'Toole, both patron saints of the Archdiocese of Dublin.

Dome of St Mary's Pro-Cathedral.

NAME	St Mary's Pro-Cathedral
ADDRESS	Cathedral and Marlborough sts, Dublin 1, Ireland
CONSTRUCTION HISTORY	**12th century** Abbey of St Mary established
	1729 St Mary's Chapel opened
	1815 Foundation stone laid of new church
	1825 Dome built; cathedral completed and dedicated
	Late 19th/20th century Interior redecorated
COMMISSIONED BY	Pastor John Linegar (St Mary's Chapel); Archbishop John Thomas Troy (Pro-cathedral)
ARCHITECT	Cathal O'Neill (redesign of sanctuary)
MATERIALS	Stone
STYLE	Greek Revival, Renaissance (interior)

St Mary's Pro-Cathedral does not yet have full cathedral status. Yet it remains an active house of worship, home to a talented choir and to national and community celebrations.

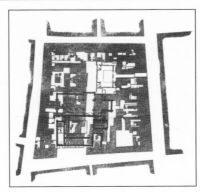

Facing page:
St Mary's Pro-Cathedral looks Grecian on the exterior but is abundantly decorated in the Victorian style within.

Monument of Cardinal Cullen, first Archbishop of Dublin.

Ravenna Cathedral

Ravenna was the capital of the Western Roman Empire when it was taken over by the Germanic Goths in the 6th century, with the support of the Byzantine emperor Justinian I. Churches were built and adorned in the lavish Byzantine style and Ravenna Cathedral is one of the great examples that exhibits the blending of the West with the Orient both in form and decoration. The royal sum of 26,000 gold pieces is said to have been spent on it, which was in all probability entirely donated by a rich banker, or Justinian himself to consolidate Byzantine rule. The cathedral was built on the site of St Vitale's martyrdom at the hands of the Roman emperor Diocletian in the 4th century (Vitale was a slave converted to Christianity by his master Agricola, who was also executed). The Byzantine-style church was completed in about 22 years and consecrated by the first archbishop of Ravenna, Maximian.

Built on an octagonal plan and not very large in size, the basilica has a two-storied ambulatory running all around covered with flat roofs. The central space is topped by a great cupola, also octagonal in shape. The upper ambulatory was traditionally used for women. The entrance, or narthex, protrudes from the west end, and a small choir and apse extend outwards on the east. Although murals decorate the cupola inside, they fade before the dazzling Byzantine mosaics in green, blue, and gold that are the real glory of the church. The main concentration of the mosaics is in the presbytery and the apse beyond. Both exhibit different styles. The former shows the influence of the Roman-Hellenistic tradition in that the figures are lively, while they are more static in the apse, a characteristic of the Byzantine school. Prophets and stories from the Old Testament, Christ and the Apostles, saints and martyrs of the Christian era, Bishops Ecclesius and Maximian, and the Emperor Justinian himself are all portrayed, and often against a background of plants and animals. The entrance arch to the presbytery is also stunningly adorned with mosaic panels.

NAME	San Vitale Basilica (Basilica di San Viatale)
ADDRESS	Via San Vitale 17, Ravenna, Italy
CONSTRUCTION HISTORY	**526 CE–548 CE** Cathedral built and consecrated
COMMISSIONED BY	Bishop Ecclesius
MATERIALS	Brick
STYLE	Byzantine

Ravenna's basilica has survived in practically pristine condition. It was copied by Charlemagne for the Palatine Chapel built in Aachen in 805 CE. Centuries later, the octagonal structure for the cupola inspired Brunelleschi's design for the famous dome of Florence Cathedral.

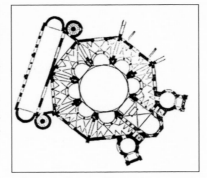

Facing page:
Based on an octagonal plan, the Ravenna basilica combines Roman and Byzantine elements.

Byzantine mosaics feature curtains which were presumably hurriedly done to replace Gothic figures.

A mosaic of Emperor Justinian with Archbishop Maximilian and Praetorian guards.

St Mark's Basilica

The apostle St Mark founded the Christian community in Alexandria. When he died a violent death in 67 CE his followers hid his body, which remained in Egypt for 800 years until it was brought by Venetian merchants surreptitiously to Venice. Here it was finally laid to rest in a church that was a temporary building in the Doge's palace. This church was replaced by a new one on the present site, which was burnt in a rebellion, and in its place the existing basilica was built. It was consecrated when St Mark's body was discovered by the Doge (elected head of the city of Venice) of the time. The canal city controlled the maritime trade of the eastern Mediterranean, and the church served as the Doge's personal chapel and also the state church.

The basilica was built on the traditional Greek cross plan and is directly modeled on the Church of the Holy Apostles in Constantinople. Venice was increasingly exposed to the eastern world through maritime trade or warfare, and the basilica, too, was increasingly subjected to decorative inputs from the Byzantium. Acquisitions by way of columns, capitals, and other sculptural items from the Orient, found a home in the basilica, which was also embellished by the work of Jacopo Sansovini. His library, next door to the cathedral, forms part of the world famous urban ensemble of the Piazza San Marco, along with the Doge's palace. The façade is a stunning composition of architectural design, paintings, and sculptures, amongst which the four horses, brought back from the Fourth Crusade in 1204 ride forth on top of the central entrance arch. Mosaics decorate the side portals while on the roofscape stand statues personifying the cardinal virtues and St Mark himself. Equally breathtaking is the interior, a glittering panorama of bright mosaics in stone, bronze, and gold.

NAME	Patriarchal Cathedral Basilica of St Mark's (Basilica di San Marco)
ADDRESS	Piazza San Marco, Venice, Italy
CONSTRUCTION HISTORY	**829–36 CE** 1st church
	976 CE 2nd church burnt; rebuilt **978 CE**
	1043–71 Present basilica built; consecrated 1094
	1343–54 Baptistery, Chapel of St Isidore built
	1423–57 Chapel of Our Lady (or of the Mascoli) built
	1523–39 Renovation of presbytery
COMMISSIONED BY	Doge Domenico Contarini
MATERIALS	Brick, marble, wooden domes
STYLE	Byzantine

Many of the figures now seen ornamenting the church are replicas of the originals which are kept in the basilica museum, such as the four horses. It was only in 1807 that St Mark's became the seat of the Archbishop of Venice, also referred to as the Patriarch of Venice.

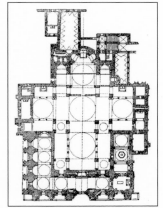

Facing page:
Façade of St Mark's Basilica from the famous Piazza San Marco.

Detail of the rooftop with St Mark and angels above the winged lion, mascot of Venice.

Painted tympanums on either side of the central portal.

123

ITALY

Pisa

Rome

Pisa Cathedral

Centerpiece of the Piazza di Duomo complex, Pisa Cathedral is one of four major monuments that have made the city a prime destination in Italy. Along with the baptistery, *campo santo* (cemetery), and *campanile* (leaning tower), it is recognized as one of the main centers for western medieval art and architecture. The cathedral is dedicated to St Mary of the Assumption. Pisa owes its importance in history to its status as a maritime power, and the cathedral became an established center of worship in the Christian world during the Romanesque period. Its wealthy status is reflected in this world-famous grouping of monuments related to Roman Catholicism. Its first bishop is recorded in 313 CE.

Resembling other basilican churches in plan, with long rows of columns connected by arches, and a nave with double aisles, the cathedral made use of the extant remains of Roman buildings. The proximity of neighboring mountains which yielded marble, alabaster, and other minerals, was a great advantage, contributing to the wealth of the city that made possible this historic complex. Four tiers of open arcades with delicate columns and Moorish type arches rise above the three bronze doors of the Classical façade ending in a gable higher than the dome itself. Columns and arches provide a supporting structure on both the exterior, where they are faced with polychrome bands of marble, and the interior. The usual entrance to the cathedral is from the south transept through a beautiful bronze door carved by Bonnano Pisano. The baptistery and tower follow the decoration pattern of the cathedral, all of which fall along the east-west axis, while the cemetery runs parallel along the enclosing wall. The nave, the apse, and cupola are decorated with mosaics and frescoes. In contrast, the rest of the interior is relatively plain.

NAME	Pisa Cathedral (Duomo di Pisa)
ADDRESS	Piazza dei Miracoli, Pisa, Italy
CONSTRUCTION HISTORY	**1063–1118** 1st phase of building; dome completed (1383 arcade around it); consecrated (1118)
	1152–1271 Baptistery begun; campanile built
	1277–14th century Cemetery built; pulpit carved
ARCHITECTS	Buscheto, Rainaldo, Dioto Salvi (Baptistery), Bonanno Pisano (campanile)
MATERIALS	Brick, stone, marble
STYLE	Romanesque

The original pulpit, a masterpiece of art, was put away after the fire of 1565, rediscovered and reassembled only in 1926. Another fire destroyed the tomb of Pope Gregory VIII, one of the notables to have been buried inside. Despite the bombing of 1944, many of the complex's original precious works survive.

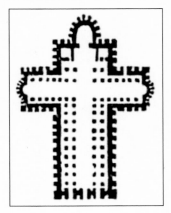

Facing page:
Pisa Cathedral, the leaning tower, and baptistery form a complex of architectural and artistic excellence.

The oval dome at the transept crossing, painted by Orazio Riminaldi.

The gilded coffer ceiling of the nave carries the coat of arms of the Medici family.

Modena Cathedral

Modena, once an ancient necropolis, was a poor little village, beset by floods every year, where the early cathedral was on the verge of collapse around 900 years ago. In 1099, however, the charismatic Matilda of Canossa, an ardent Roman Catholic, set about propagating the faith in Tuscany through building churches and monasteries, wherever possible. The new Modena cathedral was a result of one such effort. Built on the site of the sepulcher of St Geminianus, Modena's patron saint, she was fortunate in finding an architect who came from the reputed school of builders in Como. After the foundations were laid, the building progressed rapidly, stones were miraculously found to be in abundant supply, and within six years, the building was consecrated by Pope Paschal II in the presence of Matilda, and the relics of St Geminianus were transfered from the old cathedral to the new one.

Where the architect Lanfranco's skills produced a structure of classic elegance and majesty, linking it with its Roman heritage, his contemporary, the sculptor Wiligelmo, gave it subtle decorative finishes with equal precision and artistry. The Modena model was to inspire many other churches in northern Italy. The three-aisled plan without a transept, ends in a deep choir with a tripartite apse. As was the pattern in churches of the region, the bell tower—here, the famous Ghirlandina Tower—was detached from the main building. Wiligelmo's screen façade and that outside the chevet are decorated with very tall blind arcades, with little arches separating the lower and upper levels. A wide rose window is in the center between two sturdy buttresses that frame the central portal. The interior is articulated with ornamental details. A particularly engaging piece among the art works is the north portal carving of what is believed to be a scene from the Arthurian legend, *The Abduction of Guinevere*.

The deep choir with a tripartite apse.

NAME	Modena Cathedral
ADDRESS	Piazza Grande, I-41100 Modena, Italy
CONSTRUCTION HISTORY	**5th century Early** cathedral
	c. 1099–1184 Present cathedral built and consecrated
	12th–14th-century Cathedral modified;
COMMISSIONED BY	Canossa family
ARCHITECTS	Lanfranco, Wiligelmo; Anselmo da Campione (façade embellishment)
MATERIALS	Stone from old Roman monuments and quarries of Vicenza and Verona, brick interior facing
STYLE	Early Romanesque

The town has become famous for its association with famous Italian sports cars now made here—Ferrarri, Pagani, Maserati—as well as the operatic tenor Luciano Pavarotti, whose funeral was held in the cathedral in 2007 but its most enduring legacy remains the 12th-century Romanesque cathedral.

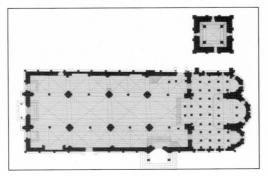

Facing page:
Modena Cathedral is a monument of striking classical beauty.

A painting of The Abduction of Guinevere.

Assisi
Rome

ITALY

Assisi Cathedral

UNESCO World Heritage Site

The first church to have been built on the site of the present cathedral probably in the 5th century was dedicated to St Rufino, the 3rd-century bishop who brought Christianity to Assisi. The second church followed a miracle believed to have occurred here. Evidence of this having been the site of a Roman forum could perhaps be traced to the fact that this church had a stout bell tower standing over a Roman cistern. Almost 100 years later, a bishop (*c.* 1134) is also said to have had a vision, guiding him to build a completely new church, in the form of the present cathedral. A high point in its history is the baptism of St Francis of Assisi which took place in its precincts.

The cathedral has two distinct styles. The two lower sections are Romanesque in their ornamentation, especially at the entrance façade and in a cornice displaying ghoulish animals. Sculptures of lions and griffins, intertwined swans, and saints also surround the entrance portal. The second level is delineated by a blind gallery and a central rose window flanked by two smaller ones. The highest level, more Gothic, is covered with a sloping roof and has a tympanum, which remains undecorated. Although the interior was remodeled later in late Renaissance style, the original barrel vaults were left untouched, though hidden by a new vaulting system. Paintings and sculptured wooden stalls add to the beauty of the three-aisled interior. The Chapel of Our Lady of Consolation was added following a reported vision of Our Lady of Sorrows weeping over Christ in her arms.

NAME	Cathedral of St Rufino (Duomo di San Rufino)
ADDRESS	Piazza San Rufino, 06081 Assisi, Umbria, Italy
CONSTRUCTION HISTORY	*c.* **5th century** 1st church
	c. **1028–36** Romanesque church and bell tower built
	1134–1253 Present cathedral built and consecrated
	15–16th century Chapels of Our Lady of Consolation and Blessed Sacrament built; interior remodeled
COMMISSIONED BY	Bishop Clarissimus
ARCHITECTS	Giovanni da Gubbio, Galeazzo Alessi (interior modified)
MATERIALS	Stone
STYLE	Romanesque (Umbrian), Gothic

In 1882 a terracotta tabernacle was presented on the occasion of the 700th anniversary of St Francis's birth. The museum and crypt of San Rufino were opened in 1941, and house a heavily gilded reliquary containing wood from the 'true cross'.

Facing page:
Assisi Cathedral has a rather austere, classical exterior giving it the appearance of a monastery.

Gilded statues and capitals in the central altar surround the illuminated image of the Virgin Mary.

Statue of the Virgin Mary with Christ in her arms.

ITALY

Rome

Monreale

Monreale Cathedral

Southern Italy and Sicily were subject to Norman, Arab, and Byzantine occupation at different periods in their history, affecting the art and architecture of the region. Monreale Cathedral superbly reflects these influences. The abbey of Monreale was built in 1174 and two years later the abbot was given the title of a bishop. Today the Roman Catholic bishop is a suffragan of the Diocese of Palermo. It was built by the Norman ruler William II as a consequence of his dream where it is said the Virgin Mary asked him to build her a church in which he should keep the state treasure that had been stolen by his father. The church was also a political statement, reinforcing the Christian faith in an atmosphere of spreading Arab influence, and an expression of William's desire to outdo the splendid Palatine Chapel built by his grandfather in nearby Palermo. The cathedral is part of a grand royal complex, built on the edge of Monreale's historic center, a small town overlooking the Oreto River.

Covering a vast area, the basilican plan of the cross vault with a single nave and three apses is decidedly Romanesque; the exterior decoration Mozarabic in design; and the golden interior is gloriously Byzantine. The nave has a timbered roof opulently covered with paintings and mosaics, several of which tell the story of Genesis. In the cloister, twin slender columns, alternately plain or decorated, arranged in plain or spiralled form, with sculptured capitals of varied design on which the Arab arches rest, create an incredible sense of transparency. The real splendor of the cathedral is its wealth of decoration, both inside and without. Foliage motifs, polychrome inlays, and chevron and chequered mosaics, paintings of kings and queens, statues of saints and apostles, and the dominant central image inside of Christ Pantocrator above the Virgin and Child make up an extraordinarily rich vocabulary of ornament and decoration.

Twin pillars around the cloister alternately ornamented with polychrome mosaics and capitals of different designs.

NAME	Monreale Cathedral (Duomo di Monreale)
ADDRESS	Piazza Vittorio Emanuele, I-90046 Monreale, Sicily, Italy
CONSTRUCTION HISTORY	**1174–85 Cathedral built and consecrated**
	1200 Cloisters built
	16th century Portico over north door
	17th–19th centuries Two Baroque chapels; west façade portico; wooden vault painted
COMMISSIONED BY	William II
MATERIALS	Stone, marble, timber roof, bronze doors
STYLE	Norman, Romanesque, Neo-Classical (west portico)

In 1811 a fire severely damaged the tombs of William I and II as well as most of the choir roof, which was restored a few years later. Two Baroque chapels were added in the 17th and 18th centuries.

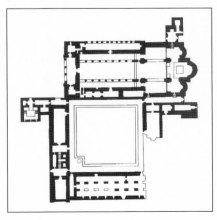

Facing page:
Monreale Cathedral is an example of architecturally diverse styles seen in both the exterior and interior.

A stunning display of Byzantine decoration on the timber roof of the nave.

Siena Cathedral

According to the famous legend of Romulus and Remus, Siena was founded by their sons. Siena Cathedral is supposedly built on the site of the Roman temple of Minerva. The first bishop is recorded in 465 CE. Siena was an independent republic in the 12th century and became prosperous as the presence of silver mines nearby attracted people with wealth, especially bankers. The 13th century saw the first attempt at expanding the existing large Romanesque cathedral by covering the nave with a dome, which could only be done by building a baptistery at the east end, that could later be extended. This plan was abandoned in favor of building another church, the Duomo Nuovo (New Cathedral), which would surpass even Rome's St Peter's, and the existing old church would then become the transept of the new one.

Although work had started on the New Cathedral, it soon came to a halt when the Black Death (plague) of 1348 hit the city. The partly built walls are a reminder of Siena's ambitious plans and one-time wealth. The older building, nevertheless presents a unified appearance due in great measure to the system of black and white bands of marble cladding both inside and on the exterior. Giovanni Pisano's west façade is a work of art said to rival that of Orvieto Cathedral. It was partly redesigned in the 19th century and again after World War II with replicas of the originals. The interior is a living museum of busts of popes, emperors, and saintly figures. An interesting feature is the marble pavement that has 56 inlaid panels illustrating Sienese history and biblical scenes, designed by individual artists.

A frontal view of the cathedral's organ.

NAME	Cathedral of Saint Mary of the Assumption (Duomo di Santa Maria dell'Assunta, Duomo di Siena)
ADDRESS	Piazza del Duomo, Siena, Tuscany, Italy
CONSTRUCTION HISTORY	**9th century** Existing Romanesque cathedral
	1215 New Cathedral begun; construction stopped 1348
	13th century Existing cathedral: pulpit, vault, transepts completed; **dome covered with** copper; lower half of façade built; consecrated (1263)
	14th century Upper half of façade, campanile completed; new nave built; façade redesigned (**1376**)
	1866–69 Façade again remodeled
ARCHITECTS	Nicola and Giovanni Pisano, Camaino di Crescentino, Gian Lorenzo Bernini (lantern on dome)
MATERIALS	White, greenish black, and red marble
STYLE	Gothic, Romanesque

At the end of the 15th century, a library was constructed off the left side of the nave, inspired by the Vatican library. The last sculptural addition to the cathedral was the small 17th-century Chigi Chapel with a gilded dome. Bernini, the young Michelangelo, and Donatello's work, along with so many others make Siena's cathedral, though unfinished, one of the most exciting treasure houses of Italian sculpture and art today.

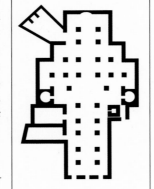

Facing page: The façade of Siena Cathedral, its central door in bronze designed by Enrico Manfrini, dating to 1958.

A large panel of the mosaic floor in the transept depicts The Slaughter of the Innocents.

Orvieto

Rome

Orvieto Cathedral

Dedicated to St Mary, Orvieto Cathedral houses the Corporal of Bolsena. This cloth dates to a miracle in nearby Bolsena, in which it was seen to be stained by reddish spots during Mass, proving the miracle of transubstantiation to a sceptic serving priest. Built over a period of 300 years, its original design as a Romanesque basilica was transformed into Italian Gothic forms. The foundation stone of the building was laid by Pope Nicholas IV in 1290, but it was not until 1309 that the Sienese architect and sculptor, Lorenzo Maitani was commissioned that several unresolved structural problems were settled, and the structure modified. He died before the completion of the cathedral, and several architects and others worked on the building, particularly the façade, keeping in mind the original ideas of Maitani.

The cruciform plan has a nave, two aisles, and six bays. Alternate rows of alabaster and travertine distinguish the lower part of both the exterior and interior, while above, black and white stripes continue in a similar alternating pattern. The Chapel of the Corporal where the Bolsena relic is kept lies on the north of the crossing and is taken out for viewing in religious processions. An almost identical chapel is that of the Madonna dedicated to San Brizio, the bishop who brought Christianity to Orvieto. The walls of the chapel and vault are covered with frescoes painted by well-known artists of the period, such as Fra Angelico and Luca Signorelli. Many of them feature grim subjects such as *The Preaching of the Antichrist* and *The End of the World* and *The Damned are taken to Hell and received by Demons.*

Black and white marble stripes cover the main body of the cathedral.

NAME	Orvieto Cathedral (Duomo di Orvieto)
ADDRESS	Piazza del Duomo, I-05018 Orvieto, Umbria, Italy
CONSTRUCTION HISTORY	*c.* 1290 Construction begun
	1309–56 Consecrated (1309); modifications to structure, apse, interior; beginning of façade; Chapel of the Corporal built
	15th century New Chapel built
	1590, 1605–07 Façade completed
COMMISSIONED BY	Pope Urban IV
ARCHITECTS	Arnolfo di Cambio, Fra Bevignate di Perugia (master mason), Lorenzo Maitani; Andrea Pisano (1347, Master of Works), Andrea di Cione (Orcagna) (1359 Master of Works), Antonio Federighi (1451–56), Michele Sanmicheli, Antonio da Sangallo, Ippolito Scalza
MATERIALS	Tufa limestone, marble, basalt, alabaster
STYLE	Romanesque, Italian Gothic

In the late 1800s a museum was made in the 13th/14th-century papal palace attached to the cathedral, which is now dedicated to the famous 20th-century sculptor Emilio Greco who made the cathedral's bronze doors. Restoration wosrk on frescoes, for which the cathedral is famous, is an ongoing process.

Facing page:
Dominating the town of Orvieto, its cathedral is a blend of styles ranging over five centuries.

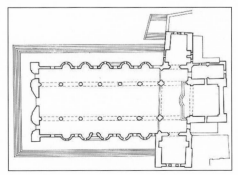

A tapestry depicts the Corporal of Bolsena displayed in a procession.

Florence Cathedral

Santa Maria del Fiore is a marvel of architecture and engineering. Even the designer of its iconic dome, Brunelleschi, appears in wonderment as his statue in the Piazza del Duomo gazes upwards towards his greatest achievement. More than 200 years in the making, the cathedral (basilica) was preceded by the 5th-century Santa Reparata. This building had become too small for the growing commercial city, and there was also the inspiration of other Tuscan cities like Pisa and Siena, which had embarked on extravagant rebuilding programs for their own cathedrals. Arnolfo di Cambio won the competition for a new design, and the project, financed by the wealthy guilds of cloth merchants and weavers, progressed until his death in 1302. Giotto was then appointed and completed the campanile. Numerous architects contributed their services until the nave was built, and the next competition was held to build the enormous dome.

Spectacular in size and appearance, Brunelleschi's design of the octagon-based structure was structurally innovative and architectonically stunning. He won another competition to construct the lantern atop the dome. Along with the multicolored campanile and the baptistery, the three structures form the complete cathedral ensemble. Arnolfo's original façade was redesigned as it was considered old fashioned but remained unbuilt until the 19th century when a third competition declared a new Neo-Gothic design suitable. The plan is of a Roman cross, and the dimensions of the cathedral so immense that the interior appears austere, with many of its original art works no longer there. However, the 44 stained-glass windows shine out brilliantly, along with Vasari's splendid fresco lining the domed ceiling.

View of the carved southern entrance highlighted against alternating black and white marble.

NAME	St Mary of the Flowers Cathedral (Cattedrale di Santa Maria del Fiore, Duomo di Firenze)
ADDRESS	Piazza del Duomo, Florence, Tuscany, Italy
CONSTRUCTION HISTORY	**1296** Present cathedral begun; nave completed **1380**
	1418 All except dome completed
	1420–36 Dome constructed; cathedral consecrated
	1587 Façade demolished
	1876–87 New façade completed
COMMISSIONED BY	Cardinal Valeriana (1st Papal Legate to Florence)
ARCHITECTS	Arnolfo di Cambio; Filippo Brunelleschi (dome); Giotto di Bondone (campanile); Francesco Talenti (apse, side chapels); Giovanni di Lapo Ghini (nave and bays); Alberto Arnoldi, Giovanni d'Ambrogio, Neri di Fioravante, Orcagna; Emilio de Fabris (new façade)
MATERIALS	Masonry, marble exterior, brick dome
STYLE	Gothic, Gothic Revival façade

Excavations between 1965–74 helped reconstruct the early history of the site where Roman houses and Santa Reparata once stood. Among several important burials to have taken place in the cathedral was that of Brunelleschi himself, who lies within a humble tomb.

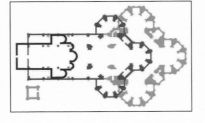

Facing page:
Named after the flower symbol of Florence, the cathedral is the city's most enduring landmark.

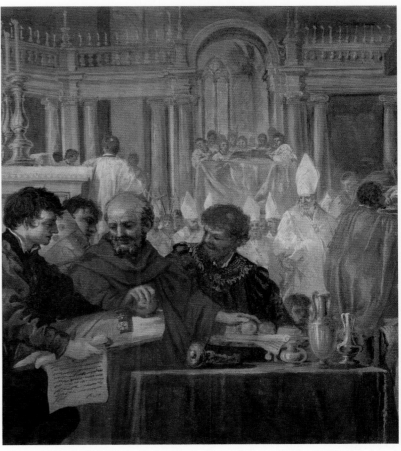

A painting titled The Mass of Leo X *inside the cathedral.*

Milan Cathedral

This Gothic masterpiece is reputed to be the second largest Catholic cathedral in the world after Seville. Dedicated to the Madonna, it took generations to build. Preceded by a Roman bath and two earlier adjoining churches, it also bears the remains of a baptistery in which St Ambrose, Bishop of Milan baptized his famous student, Augustine. The present cathedral was begun partly as a political gesture by the powerful Gian Galeazzo Visconti, first Duke of Milan, to please the working class. He also offered exclusive use of marble from his mines, exempt from taxes. In order to resolve innumerable structural problems a team of international experts was called, including the mathematician Gabriele Stornaloco. One of the reasons for the slow progress was because the cathedral's Italian designers were beset by an antagonism to foreigners. Finally Stornaloco's scheme proved sound, and the structure was eventually completed in 1572.

The colossal interior, created by the support of 52 closely spaced compound piers, contains a huge number of artworks and monuments — sarcophagi, three magnificent altars, two pulpits, statues, and paintings. However, it is the exterior which is most breathtaking with its sense of Gothic verticality. The cathedral allows visitors to walk on the marble paved roof of the nave amidst a forest of slender turrets, pinnacles, and statues. Influenced by both German and French ideas and built over so long a period of time, the cathedral lacks a certain external harmony. The overriding impression, however, is of airiness and delicacy as the rich filigree bar tracery over the walls and windows and the artistic profusion of spires dominates the whole.

A close look at the cathedral reveals repetitive patterns of bar tracery and pointed arches.

NAME	Milan Cathedral (Duomo di Milano)
ADDRESS	Piazza del Duomo, Milan, Lombardy, Italy
CONSTRUCTION HISTORY	**1075 5th and 9th century basilicas burnt down**
	1386–1402 Cathedral begun and half complete
	15th–17th century Nave and aisles built up to sixth bay (**1452**); cupola (**1500–10**); building completed (1572); consecrated (1577); west front (**1616**)
	18th/19th century Façade complete
COMMISSIONED BY	Archbishop Antonio da Saluzzo
ARCHITECTS	Simone da Orsenigo, Nicholas de Bonaventure, Jean Mignot, Pellegrino Pellegrini, Carlo Buzzi, Francesco Croce
MATERIALS	Brick faced with marble
STYLE	Gothic (Rayonnant), Gothic Revival

Large parts of the exterior decoration and façade were completed only on the insistence of Napoleon Bonaparte in the 19th century, who was crowned King of Italy at the cathedral. The last gate was inaugurated in 1965, and in 2009 renovation work on the façade finally came to an end.

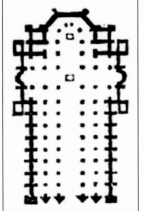

Facing page:
Pointed arches, spirals, and elongated lines of bar tracery create a Gothic wonder of ethereal majesty in Milan Cathedral.

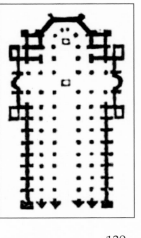

Detail of one of the gates to the Duomo.

IN HONORE... S·A·POST·PAVLVS·V·BVRGHESIVS·ROMANVS·PONT·MAX·AN·MDCXII·PONT·VII

ITALY

Rome

St Peter's Basilica

St Peter's has been hailed as "the greatest of all churches in Christendom." Probably the largest as well, it stands on the site where Peter the Apostle was crucified during the reign of Emperor Nero and buried just outside Nero's Circus, near an ancient Egyptian obelisk. St Peter is considered the first Bishop of Rome and therefore the first Pope, and St Peter's is the Pope's principal church which lies at the heart of Vatican City. Originally a flat-roofed basilica in the shape of a cross, it was centuries later, in 1506, that Pope Julius II ordered a grander building in its place.

Twenty popes reigned before the magnificent edifice was built, financed by the selling of Indulgences, a primary cause for the birth of Protestantism when Martin Luther objected to the system. The architect Bramante's design envisaged a Greek cross plan with nave, chancel, and apses, and a dome inspired by that of the Pantheon, covered by a lantern, similar to that of Florence Cathedral. Architects and engineers followed, modifying each predecessor's scheme, until in 1547 Michelangelo was appointed, unwillingly and "only for the love of God and in honor of the Apostle." Building on Bramante's plan, his special contribution was the design of the dome and chancel. Maderno, his successor, transformed the Greek cross to the Latin cross plan, by lengthening the nave; Bernini designed the imposing colonnade in front of the basilica, the narthex and portals, and baldacchino. Housing the precious *Pietà* by Michelangelo among other outstanding works of art, the interior matches the magnificent design of the entire sacred complex.

Michelangelo's Pietà *is one of the most exquisite pieces of sculpture in the world.*

NAME	St Peter's Basilica (San Pietro in Vaticano)
ADDRESS	Piazza San Pietro, Rome, Italy
CONSTRUCTION HISTORY	324 CE Original church founded
	1506 Present basilica begins
	1564–93 Dome completed
	17th century Nave begun; façade and baldacchino built; consecrated (1626); St Peter's Square completed (1656–67)
COMMISSIONED BY	Emperor Constantine
ARCHITECTS	Donato Bramante (plan), Michelangelo Buonarotti (dome), Carlo Maderno (nave, façade), Gian Lorenzo Bernini (baldacchino, colonnades)
MATERIALS	Stone, marble
STYLE	Renaissance, Paleochristian

The area now covered by Vatican City was a huge necropolis where many, including successive popes chose to be buried close to St Peter's humble shrine. In 1950 the discovery of what is believed to be St Peter's tomb ended 10 years of archaeological research under the crypt of the basilica. The most recent addition to the Vatican Grottoes was the tomb of John Paul II in 2005.

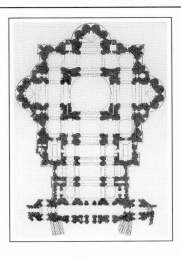

Facing page:
Dedicated to the 'prince of Apostles', St Peter's stands before a 13th-century Egyptian obelisk.

View of the interior shows the transept arms on either side and the chancel beyond the baldacchino.

Basilica of Our Lady of Guadalupe

UNESCO World Heritage Site

The Basilica of Our Lady of Guadalupe is one of the most important shrines in the Roman Catholic world, and in terms of the numbers who visit it perhaps second only to St Peter's in Rome. The cathedral honors an aspect of the Virgin Mary as she appeared to young Juan Diego, an Aztec convert, in Guadalupe, in 1531. In the vision she asked him to build a church in her honor. When asked for proof of the apparition by his bishop, Diego spread out his apron (*tilma*) in which he had gathered Castilian roses and her image was miraculously found to be imprinted on the cloth. Convinced of the truth of the vision, the bishop ordered the church to be built. The image of the Virgin has since been the lucky talisman of rebel armies, independence fighters, writers, and politicians alike.

The original church still stands on a hill north of Mexico City in Romanesque style with buttresses at either end of the façade and Doric columns inside. The new basilica had to be built when the older one could no longer accommodate the thousands who visited it to view the sacred apron that was housed here. More like a stadium, in circular form that allows the holy relic to be viewed from all angles, it stands on 350 pillars in the middle of a wide plaza. Its conical blue 'dome' sweeps upward in a slightly tilting manner to one side, so as not to compete with the domes and towers of the original basilica nearby. There are nine chapels on the first floor and another 10 under the main floor along with the crypts. The entrance is through seven front doors.

A view of the choir end of the cathedral.

NAME	Basilica of Our Lady of Guadalupe (Basílica de Nuestra Señora de Guadalupe)
ADDRESS	Paseo Zumarraga, Atrio de América, Mexico City, Mexico
CONSTRUCTION HISTORY	**1536-74** Old basilica built and consecrated (1709)
	1974-76 Present basilica built
COMMISSIONED BY	Bishop Juan de Zumárraga
ARCHITECT	Pedro Ramírez Vásquez
MATERIALS	Terracotta, stucco
STYLE	Romanesque (Old Basilica), Modern (New Basilica)

In 2003 a new plaza was added to the complex, housing a museum, auditorium, and information center. Today, despite the debates that have ensued following Juan Diego's canonization in the 1990, and without questioning the authenticity of the image, Our Lady of Guadalupe reigns as the national and religious icon of Mexico, revered through replicas of the *tilma* found all over the world.

The image of the Virgin of Guadalupe merges with that of the Pope, and is made with keys donated by Mexicans to show that they have given the Pope the keys to their hearts.

Facing page:
Millions visit the Basilica of Our Lady of Guadalupe every year to see the apron imprinted with her image.

MEXICO
Morelia
Mexico City

Morelia Cathedral

Morelia, renamed in around 1828 after a local hero who fought for Mexico's independence, is one of the great historic cities of the world. Located in central Mexico, its original name was Valladolid, given by the Spanish when they founded the city in 1541. The first church was a simple adobe and timber construction and the cathedral of the province was located at Pátzcuaro, a rival city in the province of Michoacán. It was at the end of the 16th century that political and religious power was transfered to Morelia and the cathedral was begun around 1640. It is unusual in that unlike a large number of churches in Mexico which are dedicated to the Virgin Mary, the Morelia cathedral's dedication is to the Transfiguration of Christ. The diocese of the cathedral was raised to an archdiocese in 1924.

The cathedral is surrounded by architecture from the colonial era, and plazas that were once the site of executions but have been remodeled and dignified by statues of important people in Mexico's history. It does not lie on an east-west axis, as is customary (neither does the Mexico City cathedral). It is a large building, made more impressive by the two towers that rise solidly at each end of the broad Baroque entrance façade. There are three portals, decorated with murals, with a large sculptural relief of the Transfiguration of Christ dominating the central section in white limestone. Inside, the statues and ornamentation are now distinctly Mexican or Neo-Classicist, having replaced earlier colonial era artefacts. Art treasures include a baptismal font in which the first ruler of Mexico, Agustín de Iturbide, was baptized, a gold crown gifted by Philip II of Spain, and a beautiful organ, dating to 1905.

NAME	Cathedral of the Divine Savior
ADDRESS	Morelia, Mexico
CONSTRUCTION HISTORY	*c.* **1577** 1st church built
	c. **mid 17th–mid 18th century** Present cathedral built; consecrated 1705
ARCHITECT	Vicenzo Barraso de la Escayola
MATERIALS	Pink volcanic stone
STYLE	Neo-Classical, Herreresque, Baroque

Morelia's city center was declared a UNESCO World Heritage Site in 1991 because of the "masterly and eclectic blend of the medieval spirit with Renaissance, Baroque, and Neo-Classical elements."

Facing page:
A white limestone figure of Christ dominates the central portal of Morelia Cathedral.

Mosaic tiling emphasizes the structural details of the pink stone exterior.

The baldachin under the central nave of the high vaulted interior.

St John's Cathedral

The city of 's-Hertogenbosch, popularly known as Den Bosch, was the capital of the Duke of Brabant who founded it in 1185. As it prospered, it acquired the status of an independent Roman Catholic bishopric around the mid 16th century, and the first parish church was raised to cathedral status. During the rise of Protestanism, Den Bosch supported the Roman Catholic Habsburgs, and the cathedral was shorn of most of its decorative details. It became part of the United Kingdom of the Netherlands in 1629 when the church was re-established as a Reformed Church. It was reverted to its Roman Catholic status by Napoleon after his victory over the Netherlands in 1810, and a few decades later, restoration work began in earnest on the cathedral.

Originally Romanesque in style, the cathedral was transformed to what is called the 'Brabant Gothic' of the Low Countries. With its multiple spires and chapels it has been likened to a 'mountain range rather than a church' in appearance. Originally funds were provided by merchant citizens but when the money ran short the work stopped midway. It was renewed only from the mid 19th century onwards. The cruciform plan has five naves and a single transept. Of the few artefacts that remain in the vast interior, the altar is notable for its lifelike image of the Virgin Mary grieving at the suffering of Christ. The chapel of Brotherhood of Our Lady is another work of art. Sint Janskathedraal (as the church is locally known) is also remarkable for the bright quality of light that streams in from its wide windows.

NAME	St John's Cathedral (Sint-Janskathedraal)
ADDRESS	's-Hertogenbosch, North Brabant, Netherlands
CONSTRUCTION HISTORY	**1220–1340** 1st Romanesque church built; Gothic extension of present cathedral begun (1340)
	15th century Transept, choir, Chapel of Brotherhood of Our Lady built
	1505 Romanesque church demolished except for tower
	1525 Main body of cathedral built; fire burns down tower at the crossing in 1584
	1830 Fire damages western tower, repaired in 1842
	1859–1984 Repair and restoration works
COMMISSIONED BY	Duke Henry I of Brabant
ARCHITECT	Willem von Kessels
MATERIALS	Stone
STYLE	Gothic

Thousands of pilgrims visit the statue of Our Sweet Lady of Den Bosch to seek her miraculous powers of healing. Conservation work on the weathered exterior is an ongoing process.

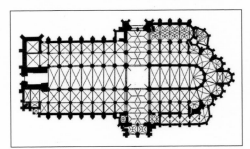

Facing page:
Bordered with innumerable spires, St John's appears like a mountain range.

Statues on the flying buttresses for which the cathedral is famous.

Decorations on the ceiling of the cathedral.

ChristChurch Cathedral

The town of Christchurch, on New Zealand's South Island, was established in 1850. In 1856, the first bishop, Henry Harper, arrived, and initiated plans for the building of a cathedral. Despite a population of a mere 450 at the time, the project nevertheless generated great enthusiasm. The acclaimed English Gothic architect, George Gilbert Scott, was commissioned and drew up plans with the help of the local architect, Robert Speechley. The foundation stone of the Anglican cathedral was laid in 1864 amidst much fanfare, but lack of funds delayed construction, causing many to discredit the project as an "honest, high-toned idea" but a "huge record of failure." In 1873 a new architect remodeled Scott's plan, and by 1881 the main body of the cathedral was completed.

Standing in the center of the city, which was originally swampy land, the cathedral was, surprisingly, planned as a wooden construction. However, the discovery of good-quality masonry stone nearby resulted in a change in structural details and building material. Each section of the cathedral has a story to tell: the panels in the west porch detail the city's history; the Pacific Chapel marks the martyrdom of the first bishop of Melanesia (now part of the Christchurch diocese); the High Altar was given in thanksgiving for a safe voyage from England by the Scottish surgeon James Irving, who arrived in Lyttleton with his family in 1879.

The rose window stands out against the gray wall surface.

NAME	ChristChurch Cathedral
ADDRESS	Cathedral Square, Christchurch Central City, New Zealand
CONSTRUCTION HISTORY	1864 Construction begun
	1881 Nave, spire completed
	1901 Spire rebuilt after damage in earthquake
	1904 Main body of cathedral complete
	1949 Memorial Chapel of St Michael and St George
ARCHITECTS	George Gilbert Scott, Benjamin Mountfort (supervisory architect)
MATERIALS	Local stone, timber roof supports
STYLE	Gothic Revival

All sections of the cathedral were finally completed by 1904, with a visitors' center following 90 years later. The stone spire was replaced with weathered copper sheeting. The latest renovations included removal of the original slate roof tiles.

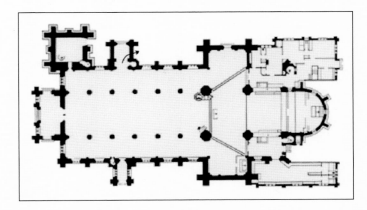

Facing page:
ChristChurch Cathedral is an attractive landmark in the center of the city

The organ was installed in 1882 and rebuilt in 1977.

ECCE TABERNACULUM DEI CUM HOMINIBUS.

CATHEDRAL OF THE BLESSED SACRAMENT

Cathedral of the Blessed Sacrament

George Bernard Shaw called it a "New Zealand Brunelleschi" and indeed, the Roman Catholic basilica in Christchurch is a magnificent Renaissance style building. Surpassing all of Francis Petre's other ecclesiastical works, it has been likened to several other cathedrals, including St Paul's in London. The site was originally occupied by a tiny pre-fabricated wooden church that served the spiritual needs of a handful of Roman Catholics. This Church of the Blessed Sacrament was opened in 1864 but on expanding, had to be physically shifted to Ferry Road—an unusual achievement. It was the dream come true of the first bishop of the Roman Catholic Diocese of Christchurch, John Joseph Grimes, for a larger cathedral that would represent the vibrant young community of the growing city. Despite problems in finding the right stone and sufficient funds, it was officially opened within four years of its founding.

Only fifty men—a large number for those days—were employed in the construction, which used huge amounts of steel, concrete, and stone. Though generally based on the style of the classic Roman basilicas, Petre's plan diverged from the convention of placing the dome over the crossing of the nave and transepts. Instead, it was positioned over the sanctuary, thus creating one vast, simple, and impressive space inside. The galleries and aisles all convey openness, and the sense of visual drama climaxing at the High Altar is intensified by the grandeur of the Byzantine apse. Ionic columns, twin towers soaring up at the entrance façade, and the green copper-roofed dome completes the imagery of the great European renaissance churches on which this is modeled.

The nave opens out like open arms to welcome the worshippers.

NAME	Cathedral of the Blessed Sacrament
ADDRESS	Barbadoes St, Christchurch, New Zealand
CONSTRUCTION HISTORY	**1864–77** Church built on site; major additions completed
	1900–05 Church (pro-cathedral) shifted to Ferry Rd; redesigned; opened 1905
	1970–2000 Conservation work; tabernacle doors dedicated; forecourt established
ARCHITECT	Francis W Petre
MATERIALS	Concrete, sheathed in Oamuru limestone
STYLE	Neo-Classical; Byzantine apse

Considerable damage caused by atmospheric pollution from a nearby gas works and railways required a thorough cleaning job in the 1970s. Along with this, the interior was altered to reflect the changing liturgical needs of recent times. Various local artists have contributed to the interior features, such as the tabernacle doors, the stained-glass window in the Lady Chapel, the Crucifix, and the new Stations of the Cross.

Facing page:
Designed in the Italian basilica style the cathedral's Ionic columns lend majesty to the façade.

Detail of the ceiling above the center of the church.

Cathedral of St Paul

The Anglican Diocese of Wellington was established in 1858, almost a century before construction of its cathedral began. However, even before that, in the 1840s, the Anglican community of the city had started collecting bricks for a church. At the time of construction in 1955, however, a major earthquake convinced the community of the undesirability of a brick construction in the area. The two predecessors to the present cathedral had both been made of timber, the first in Thorndon, which the early settlers had built, and the second, still referred to as Old St Paul's, in Mulgrave Street nearby. It was always understood by the community that the latter building was only a temporary home but Old St Paul's in fact functioned as the seat of the bishop for 98 years. Lack of finances brought on by World War I delayed plans for the new building. Eventually, despite the further setbacks of World War II, land was purchased and funds raised to build half the cathedral.

The original plan was based on the great medieval stone cathedrals of Europe. However, the greater durability of strong, reinforced concrete that would withstand the hazards of an earthquake prone region, caused changes in the architecture. A simple, sturdy structure, without undue embellishment was designed by Cecil Wood and completed 60 years later by his protégé, Miles Warren. Services began in a half-completed church in the white marble-floored sanctuary. The nave was extended only during the second stage of work, beginning in 1970. Several local artists and craftspersons contributed, including a seven-year-old embroiderer. A precious addition was a historic wooden structure, formerly at the church in Paraparaumu, and now consecrated as the Lady Chapel.

Contemporary artists and crafts people from New Zealand have contributed to the art works inside.

NAME	Cathedral of St Paul
ADDRESS	45 Molesworth St, Thorndon 6011, Wellington, New Zealand
CONSTRUCTION HISTORY	**Before 1855** 1st church of St Paul's
	1865 2nd church (Old St Paul's); consecrated 1866
	1955–**64** Present cathedral begun and 1st stage completed; consecrated; **1972** 2nd stage completed
	1991–98 Lady Chapel added; cathedral completed
ARCHITECTS	Cecil Wood, Miles Warren
MATERIALS	Reinforced concrete
STYLE	Modern

In the late 1990s additional funds were raised to complete the building, which included the portal and a commemorative tower. Finally in 1998, the finished cathedral was dedicated by the tenth Bishop of Wellington.

Facing page:
Built in three stages, the modern looking Wellington Cathedral is an impressive structure without undue embellishments.

The Holm Window, designed by a leading New Zealand stained-glass artist.

NORWAY

Trondheim

Oslo

Nidaros Cathedral

Housing the relics of Olav Haraldsson, a Norwegian king and saint, the Nidaros Lutheran cathedral is the most important church and place of pilgrimage in Norway. A Viking man of war he converted to Christianity in England, and returned to Norway to rule and propagate the faith. However, forced into exile by jealous rivals, he again returned but was killed in battle near Trondheim in 1030. He was proclaimed a martyr by his followers, and accorded the status of a saint, in whose name miracles occurred. A small chapel was built over his grave in which his relics were kept. It was over this that the first cathedral, called Christchurch, was built by Olav's nephew. This gave place to the present building when the need for more space arose to accommodate the growing numbers of the faithful.

Nidaros became an archbishopric in 1152 and work proceeded steadily with English masons on the new cathedral until Archbishop Øystein was sent to England, where he came under the influence of the new and popular Gothic style. On his return he set about adding Gothic elements to the church with the help of French masons. The nave was extended westward to end in a grand western façade. Periodic fires over the next 400 years resulted in many reconstructions. The influence of English cathedrals of the time is apparent, as is Reims Cathedral in the sculptures. The altarpiece is remarkable, depicting the legend of St Olav. However, nearly all the original artworks have been lost or destroyed except for a silver chalice and a large chest; the rest are replicas.

The entrance doorway.

NAME	Nidaros Cathedral (Nidarosdomen, Trondheim Cathedral)
ADDRESS	Trondheim, Norway
CONSTRUCTION HISTORY	*c.* **1070–90** Christchurch built on site of 1st wooden chapel
	1152 Present cathedral begun; transept, Chapter House part nave completed
	12th–13th century New presbytery, Gothic choir built; nave extended
	1300 Cathedral built
	1869–1969 Nave rebuilt
COMMISSIONED BY	King Olav the Gentle (1st church); Bishops Jon and Øystein Erlendsson (Gothic expansion till transept); Archbishop Sigurd (nave extension and west front)
ARCHITECTS	After 1869 Heinrich Ernst Schirmer, Christian Christie
MATERIALS	Stone
STYLE	Anglo-Norman, Romanesque, Early Gothic

The tombs of several monarchs lie in the crypt. Major rebuilding started in the 20th century and the cathedral was officially declared complete in 2001.

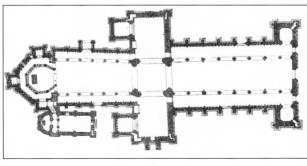

Facing page: Standing out in the stark Norwegian landscape, Nidaros Cathedral is an elegant vision of medieval architecture.

Sculpture-filled niches on the west front display figures of apostles, saints, bishops, angels, and saintly virtues.

POLAND

Poznan   Warsaw

Poznan Cathedral

Initially dedicated only to St Peter, Poznań Cathedral has its origins in the first 10th-century church on the site, which was raised to the status of a cathedral when Bishop Jordan was sent to Poland, probably on the orders of the Pope. This building was also where Mieszko I, considered the de facto creator of the Polish state, was baptized when he converted to Christianity. He is reputed to be the builder of a three-aisled church. This cathedral was rebuilt twice before its final Neo-Classical rebirth after a major fire in 1772. In 1821 Pope Pius VII raised it to the status of a metropolitan archcathedral, at the same time rededicating it to St Paul along with St Peter.

The extant remains of earlier structures are apparent in either the basement (pre-Romanesque first cathedral), southern tower (Romanesque second cathedral), or sections of the Gothic, or Neo-Classical remodelings. During its Gothic incarnation, which is also the most interesting architecturally, a new presbytery with a chevet and chapels was added. The front façade is entirely Gothic, with a rose window and gables above the portals. Constructed in the form of a basilica without transepts, the interior of the eastern end vaults upward, creating a continuous vast space from the High Altar up to the clerestories and ending at the apex of the vault. The huge space is illuminated by the light that pours in from the elongated stained-glass windows atop the ambulatory. From Gothic sculptures to Flemish tapestries, to the tombstones that are largely Renaissance in style, there is a rich mix of art and craftsmanship.

NAME	Archcathedral Basilica of St Peter and St Paul
ADDRESS	Ostrów Tumski 17, Poznań, Poland
CONSTRUCTION HISTORY	**10th–11th century** 1st and 2nd churches
	13th–15th century Present cathedral built
	1622 Fire; rebuilt 17th century
	1722 Fire; façade rebuilt (1779)
COMMISSIONED BY	Mieszko I
ARCHITECTS	Pompeo, Antoni Ferrari (17th century, Baroque); Efraim Schroeger (façade 1779); Bonaventura Solari (cupolas 1790); Franciszek Morawski (reconstruction 1945–56)
MATERIALS	Brick
STYLE	Romanesque, Gothic

Much of the Gothic reconstruction was later done over with Baroque and Neo-Classical features and even this was destroyed during World War II. Today's cathedral is largely a reconstruction that approximates the original Gothic design.

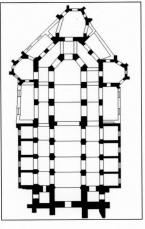

Brick has been exploited in a colorful way in this entrance portal.

The epitaph of a suffragan bishop of Poznan bears the Lodzia coat of arms.

Facing page:
Behind its Gothic front façade the Romanesque origins of Poznań's cathedral are visible in its southern end.

POLAND

Warsaw

Krakow

Wawel Cathedral

With 1000 years of history behind it, Wawel Cathedral is perhaps the most important national monument in Poland. It has been the coronation site of 37 Polish monarchs as well as the burial ground of royalty and other national figures (even after the capital moved to Warsaw), including the bishops of Krakow. In contemporary history it is best associated with Pope John Paul II, who offered his first Mass here in the crypt in 1946 and later served as Archbishop of Krakow before his papal appointment. The Roman Catholic cathedral of the Archdiocese of Krakow is the third church to be built on the site and is dedicated to St Stanislas, a devout Jesuit and Poland's patron saint. Located on Wawel Hill, which has been a tribal stronghold since the 10th century, it stands inside the castle by the same name.

Largely in the same condition as it was when built, the cathedral has a somber ambience, austere in the exterior, and rather gloomy within. Of the three towers, the Sigismund tower is the most famous. The cathedral's most attractive features are the 18 radiating chapels full of religious art that have been built around the ambulatory. Among these are the Waza and Sigismund chapels, the latter built by the Florentine architect Bartolomeo Berrecci. It is a gem of Renaissance design. Covered by a golden dome it is the funerary chapel for some of the Grand Dukes of Lithuania and kings of Poland. Underneath the canopy of the main altar is a replica of the silver coffin of St Sigismund.

A detail from the Waza Chapel.

NAME	Cathedral Basilica of Ss Stanislas and Wenceslas (Wawel Cathedral, Katedra Wawelska)
ADDRESS	Wawel 15, Wawel Castle, Krakow 31-001, Poland
CONSTRUCTION HISTORY	**11th–12th century** 1st and 2nd church (burnt 1305)
	12th century St Leonard's crypt built
	1320–64 Present cathedral built and consecrated
	1517–33 Sigismund Chapel built
	c. **1650** High Altar (Baroque) built
COMMISSIONED BY	Bishop Jan Muskata
ARCHITECT	Bartolomeo Berrecci (Sigismund Chapel)
MATERIALS	Stone, black and rose marble
STYLE	Gothic, Renaissance (Sigismund's Chapel)

Altered over time as new burial chapels were added and the interior refurbished in the 17th century with a Baroque touch, the eastern end of the cathedral changed somewhat from the original plan. Wawel Cathedral remains a place of pilgrimage and venue for significant national events.

An early 20th-century mural in St Sophia's Chapel.

Facing page:
Located on Wawel Hill, the cathedral is popularly known for its association with Pope John Paul II.

PORTUGAL

Braga

Lisbon

Braga Cathedral

Christianity came to northern Portugal in the 3rd century, and Braga was one of the oldest dioceses on the Iberian peninsula. The migrant Germanic tribe, the Suebis, had made Braga their capital and were subsequently converted to Christianity in the 6th century, but the town lost its bishopric with the Arab invasion. It was almost four centuries later that the bishopric was restored, and a cathedral was built but only up to the eastern chapels. It was consecrated in 1089. Later, Henry of Burgundy and his consort Dona Teresa persuaded the Pope to support further construction, which continued until the 12th century.

This three-aisled cathedral with a transept and five chapels has an imposing western entrance, with a central Romanesque arch, flanked by two others in Gothic style. Its original design was influenced by the monastery church of Cluny but later additions and modifications gave it a more eclectic vocabulary, which included the local Portuguese Manueline, and the Baroque. Behind the projecting portals and the entrance gallery, the body of the cathedral rises high, with minimal decoration and window openings. Above this solid exterior, squat towers on either side with many-armed Baroque spires meeting in a gesture like the joining of hands. Lodged between the towers is a niche bearing a larger than life statue of the Mother and Child. The cathedral's Manueline features are most apparent in the main chapel—its tracery, vaulting, and statuary. Typical blue-white tiles in the chapel of St Peter of Rates lend a regional touch while the Chapel of the Glory displays Moorish geometrical motifs. The nave retains its Romanesque elements even though most of the original capitals of the columns are lost.

Devoid of excessive decoration, the nave offers a clear view of the High Altar.

NAME	Braga Cathedral (Sé de Braga)
ADDRESS	Rua Dom Paio Mendez, Braga, Portugal
CONSTRUCTION HISTORY	*c.* **1071–12th century** Cathedral built up to eastern chapels; consecrated 1089
	14th century Chapel of the Kings, Chapel of the Glory built
	15th-16th century Entrance gallery, main chapel, Chapel of Piety built
	17th century Towers and upper stories completed
COMMISSIONED BY	Count Henry of Burgundy and Dona Teresa
MATERIALS	Stone, timber roof of apse and aisles
STYLE	Romanesque, Manueline, Gothic, Baroque

The cathedral museum has some interesting works of art, especially the 18th-century choir stalls. The last rebuilding took place in the 19th century when the cloisters were altered.

Facing page:
Originally Romaesque, Braga Cathedral includes chapels in the Manueline and Baroque styles.

An ironwork detail illustrates the excellence of local craftsmanship.

PORTUGAL

Lisbon

Lisbon Cathedral

Lisbon, historically known as Olissipo when it was part of the Roman Empire, was one of the early cities to be converted to Christianity. History records its conquest by the Moors in the 8th century who brought prosperity to the city. Though Islam was now dominant, Christians were allowed to keep their religion, but it was the Reconquista, led by Alfonso I of Portugal, which finally established Roman Catholicism in the 12th century in the country. Mosques were reportedly reconverted to churches and though legend says that the city's cathedral is also built over a mosque there is no archaeological evidence to support this. The threat of repeated invasions in its history lent the ecclesiastical structure the appearance of a fortress (as in other Portuguese cathedrals), and as the city grew, being a focal point for commerce, the cathedral was patronized and expanded through the centuries.

The cathedral is built on the cruciform plan with three aisles, transepts, and a main chapel surrounded by an ambulatory with radiating polygonal chapels. It follows the classical design of a barrel-vaulted nave with an upper arched gallery, and the entrance façade to the west with its signature rose window. Crenelated towers rise on either side. The cloister, connected to the eastern transept, was a later addition, built under the instructions of King Dinis in Gothic style. The introduction of Gothic details is also seen in the main chapel and ambulatory, which took the place of the earlier Romanesque apse and from which several other chapels radiated. The tombs of important personages are contained in the ambulatory, all bearing their coat of arms.

The Gothic cloister of Lisbon Cathedral in which each oculum over the twin arches has a different tracery pattern.

NAME	Cathedral of Santa Maria (Santa Maior de Lisboa, Sé Patriarcal, Sé de Lisboa)
ADDRESS	Largo da Sé, Lisbon, Portugal
CONSTRUCTION HISTORY	*c.* **1150−13th century** Cathedral built
	1279−325 Cloisters added
	14th century New east end built after earthquake; funerary chapel of merchant Bartolomeu Joanes added
	1755 Earthquake results in rebuilding
MATERIALS	Brick, stone
STYLE	Romanesque

A major earthquake in 1755 damaged several parts of the cathedral, causing extensive rebuilding. The main chapel now acquired Neo-Classical and Rococo details and a new sacristy was built in the Baroque style. However, most of these later decorative details were removed in the 20th century and the cathedral was restored to its original stern and heavy persona.

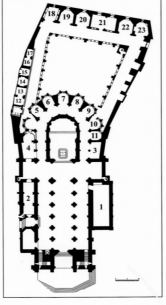

Facing page:
Crenelated towers rise over the colorful roofscape surrounding Lisbon Cathedral.

A vaulted dome with painted ceilings and exquisite wrought-ironwork in front of the organ in the main chapel.

PORTUGAL

Lisbon • • Évora

Evora Cathedral

UNESCO World Heritage Site

Evora, a town in the western Iberian peninsula, was a Roman settlement, which grew in importance probably because of the presence of gold, and because it lay at the crossroads of several significant trade routes. The earliest bishop recorded here was Quintianus in the 4th century. After it came under Visigothic rule, it is said to have become a cathedral city but not much is known about that period. Later it came under the Moors, when it received a spurt in growth but only when it was reconquered by Gerald the Fearless, was Christianity reinstated. Under King Alfonso I it became established as a Portuguese city (c. 1166) and the first known cathedral probably dates to this period, dedicated to the Virgin Mary. In 1540 it became the established seat of the archbishopric but already in 1497, Vasco da Gama is said to have invoked the blessings of the cathedral's patrons before setting out on his first expedition to the Orient.

The fortress-like cathedral of Evora stands on the highest point of the town, and like other medieval Portuguese buildings, it had Romanesque beginnings. As additions were made, it developed Gothic, Baroque, and Manueline features. A notable element is the front façade in rose granite. Wide steps leads to the semi-enclosed entrance gallery, above which can be seen the main rose window. Rose windows are also embedded in the transept outer walls. Another arresting feature is the lantern tower at the crossing surrounded by six turrets, each a miniature of the tower itself. The two towers surmounting the entrance are also interesting as they are quite dissimilar to each other in elevation. Barrel-vaulted inside, the central nave leads to a Baroque altar, the Manueline choir, and main chapel, also a beautiful Baroque work of art in polychrome marble.

NAME	Evora Cathedral (Sé de Évora)
ADDRESS	R. da República, Évora 7005, Portugal
CONSTRUCTION HISTORY	**1186–1204** Cathedral built, with towers
	1280–1340 Gothic expansion
	14th century Cloisters built
	16th century Chapel of the Esporão, two towers built
	18th century Main chapel, High Altar built
ARCHITECT	Friedrich Ludwig (main chapel, choir)
MATERIALS	Brick, rose granite (main façade), marble (High Altar)
STYLE	Romanesque, Gothic, Baroque

The cathedral's collection of art treasures includes a 17th-century reliquary supposedly containing pieces from Christ's Cross. Evora Cathedral's School of Polyphony was famous in the 16th and 17th centuries, patronized by the country's best known musicians.

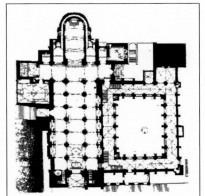

Facing page:
The main façade of Evora Cathedral in rose granite with a stepped back portal and entrance gallery.

Corridor with a sarcophagus in one of the cloister galleries.

Statues of the Apostles in the main portal of the cathedral.

Moscow   RUSSIA

St Basil's Cathedral

Formally called Cathedral of Intercession of Theotokos on the Moat, and originally the Trinity Church, St Basil's was built to commemorate the capture of the Tatar strongholds of Kazan and Astrakhan in the mid 16th century by Ivan the Terrible. After each victory in the war, Ivan added a church next to the central Church of Intercession, until the cluster became a sum of eight side churches arranged around the ninth. The cathedral acquired its present name after Basil the Blessed (1468–1552), an eccentric saint of the 'Holy Fool of Christ' type was buried here.

The building's design, shaped as a flame of a bonfire rising into the sky, has no similarities with past, contemporary, or later traditional architecture of the region. Its vivid hues reflect the changing Russian preference from the 17th century onwards for bright colors. Compared with the exotic exteriors the interiors are dark and simple. The walls are decorated with faded flower frescoes. The main chapel contains a 19th-century Baroque iconostasis. Amongst the various sanctuaries is that of the Holy Trinity, at the site where the first church stood. Others are dedicated to the saints Gregory the Illuminator, Alexander Svirsky, and Barlaam. A column commemorates the miraculous finding of an icon of St Nicholas from the Velikaya River.

Detail of a fresco on an interior wall.

NAME	Cathedral of Intercession of Most Holy Theotokos on the Moat, Temple of Basil the Blessed
ADDRESS	Red Square, Moscow, Russia
CONSTRUCTION HISTORY	**1555** Contruction begun of 1st church; consecrated 1561
	1588 10th church built over Basil's grave
	1680–83 Most significant rebuilding and expansion
	1761–84 Decoration on floors and walls
	1848 Domes colored
COMMISSIONED BY	Ivan the Terrible
ARCHITECT	Postnik Yakovlyev
MATERIALS	White stone (foundation), brick; domes crowned in gold
STYLE	Russian Byzantine, vernacular wooden architecture

In 1923 the cathedral was turned into a public museum dedicated to the Russian conquest of Tatar strongholds. Exhibits include examples of 16th-century Russian and Tatar weaponry. After Lenin's death in 1924, St Basil's almost fell victim to Josef Stalin, because it obstructed his urbanist plans for expansion but was saved from demolition. A massive restoration of the cathedral was carried out after World War II and completed in 2008, when one of sanctuaries was opened.

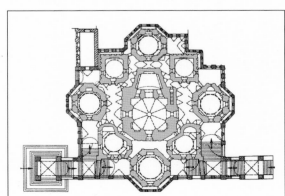

Facing page:
St Basil's is crowned with onion domes associated with Russian Orthodox churches. The shrine of the saint lies below the lowest dome on the right of the cluster.

A dazzling decorative display on one of the chapels.

St Petersburg

Moscow

RUSSIA

St Petersburg Cathedral

UNESCO World Heritage Site

Before the present St Isaac's Cathedral was commissioned, an earlier structure had been designed by the Italian architect Antonio Rinaldi. A master of the Neo-Classicist style, his cathedral was partially completed at the start of the 19th century by another Italian architect. A few years later Tsar Alexander I decided to rebuild it. After examining several designs, that by the French architect Auguste de Montferrand was chosen. He had been a student of Napoleon's designer Charles Percier, who was a proponent of what was known as the Empire style. Although initially Montferrand's grandiose scheme was heavily criticized for being too ponderous, it found favor with the tsar and work began, supervised by Montferrand himself until his death in 1858. Under the Soviets the cathedral was turned into a museum of atheism but with the disintegration of the Soviet Union, it reverted to its original status of a cathedral.

The traditional Byzantine Greek cross plan, common to Russian cathedrals, is used here too, which features a large central dome surrounded by smaller ones at each corner. The most prominent elements are the 112 red granite columns with Corinthian capitals, decreasing in number as they ascend to the level of the domes. The positioning of the columns was a great technological achievement which took more than a decade to complete and involved the use of a complicated timber framework. The cathedral itself stands on a bed of about 10,000 tree trunks, being located on marshy ground. Inside, a dozen gilded statues of angels, each six meters high, circle the rotunda. Montferrand also developed a new triple dome system, reducing both the material and costs involved. Replicas of paintings in mosaic form fill the interior, while structural elements are designed in different shades of marble and granite.

NAME	St Isaac's Cathedral (Isaakievsky Sobor, St Petersburg Cathedral)
ADDRESS	1 Isaakievskaya Place, St Petersburg, Russia
CONSTRUCTION HISTORY	**1768–1802** 1st church built
	1818–58 Present cathedral built
COMMISSIONED BY	Tsar Alexander I
ARCHITECT	Auguste de Montferrand
MATERIALS	Brick, gray and pink stone, red granite columns
STYLE	Neo-Classical/Byzantine

The cathedral was little harmed during World War II. The gilded dome was painted over in gray to camouflage it, and it was used to position a geodesical instrument which could sight the enemy. Today, the main body of the cathedral is used only on feast days and only the chapel on the left is used for regular worship.

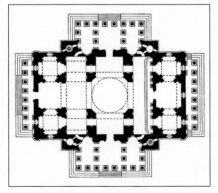

Statue of the apostle Matthew with an angel.

Interior of the great dome honoring the Holy Spirit.

Facing page:
St Isaac's Cathedral was built in the so-called Empire style for the tsars of Russia.

Cathedral of Christ the Savior

UNESCO World Heritage Site

The magnificent Cathedral of Christ the Savior built in the heart of Moscow has a colorful history. Its first manifestation dates to Napoleon's retreat from Russia, and Tsar Alexander I's decision to build a cathedral in celebration of his country's victory. It was to be based on the Hagia Sophia of Constantinople. Construction actually began under his brother and successor, Tsar Nicholas, after a convent and church were relocated from the site. The architects of Russia's Revolution in 1917 had other plans, however, and dynamited the religious structure with plans for a gigantic monument to socialism to take its place. This did not happen due to lack of funds, and under Nikita Khrushchev in the latter part of the century, a swimming pool filled up the vacant area. With the collapse of the Soviet Union in 1990 and a dynamic liberalization of Russian polity, the importance of the cathedral was once again recognized and permission was granted for it to be rebuilt.

The cathedral visualized by Tsar Nicholas was of a Neo-Classical design but was eventually built as an opulent Byzantine edifice. It took over 40 years to complete with the surrounding landscaping and interior decoration also finished by then. The tsars themselves oversaw its building and engaged the foremost architects and fresco painters of the time. It was planned as a cross with equal sides and consecrated the day Alexander III was crowned. It was also a center of learning where the best religious teachers preached and charitable works were conducted. The present cathedral faithfully follows the plan of its predecessor. However, when its restorer Alexei Denisov was replaced, several changes in the details took place. Around the central gilded dome are four smaller exact replicas, and rising high above each, is a gigantic cross. On the lowest level is an assembly hall.

NAME	Cathedral of Christ the Savior (Khram Khrista Spasitela)
ADDRESS	Central Federal District, Moscow, Russia
CONSTRUCTION HISTORY	**1839–83** 1st cathedral built; consecrated 1883; demolished 1931
	1994 Present cathedral foundations laid
	1996, 2000 Consecrated
COMMISSIONED BY	Tsar Alexander I
ARCHITECTS	Konstantin Thon (1st cathedral); Alexei M Denisov, Mikhail Mikhailovich Posokhin (present cathedral)
MATERIALS	Granite, marble
STYLE	Russian Orthodox

Today, surrounding the cathedral in the square outside are several chapels of the same design as the main building. The complete church was consecrated in 2000 although the lower part, when complete, was consecrated four years earlier.

Facing page:
A glowing example of the Russian Orthodox style, the cathedral was where the last Russian tsar and his family were revered as saints.

Detail of statues beside a cluster of lamps inside the cathedral.

Oil painting of Prince Alexander Nevsky receiving the papal legates.

St Giles Cathedral

UNESCO World Heritage Site

St Giles, to whom the cathedral, or more correctly, the kirk, is dedicated, was a 7th-century French abbot who became the patron saint of Edinburgh. Legend says he saved a deer from being wounded by an arrow by deflecting it to his own body—this incident is portrayed in the tympanum above the entrance to the cathedral. The existing building owes it origins to the Scottish royal family in the 12th century, and was Romanesque in style. It was partially burnt down in 1385, following which it was expanded piecemeal through the years. It became a cathedral when the first bishop of Edinburgh was appointed in 1635 but formally functioned as such only briefly. It was here that John Knox, looked upon as Scotland's Martin Luther, passionately preached his sermons on the Reformation. Retaining the Scottish traditional title of High Kirk, it is considered the mother church of the Established Church of Scotland.

Broadly rectangular in plan, not much remains of its 12th-century construction except for four huge central pillars. Following the Reformation the interior was segregated by internal walls and evolved into four churches and other public institutions. All around it chapels were added, which are now commonly referred to as aisles. By the 15th century as many as 50 altars existed. Following a period of neglect for almost 200 years, the exterior was restored in the early 1800s. Through the 19th century many of the minor chapels were removed and the interior opened up again. Most of the stained-glass windows were added at that time.

NAME	St Giles Cathedral (High Kirk of St Giles)
ADDRESS	High Street, Royal Mile, Edinburgh, Scotland
CONSTRUCTION HISTORY	**854 CE** Parish church built on site
	1120s-1243 Present church built and consecrated
	1385 Partly burnt; rebuilding begun
	1500 Tower heightened and stone crown added
	19th century Major restoration works
CONSECRATED	1243
COMMISSIONED BY	King David I
ARCHITECTS	William Burn (19th-century restoration); Robert Lorimer (Thistle Chapel)
MATERIALS	Stone
STYLE	Romanesque, Gothic

The 1900s saw major changes to the building. The richly decorated Thistle Chapel, dedicated to distinguished Scotsmen, was added. The focus of worship was shifted to the center, so the congregation now sits all around the High Altar.

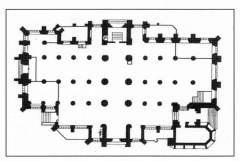

Facing page: St Giles Cathedral has a strong Gothic exterior with a unity of expression.

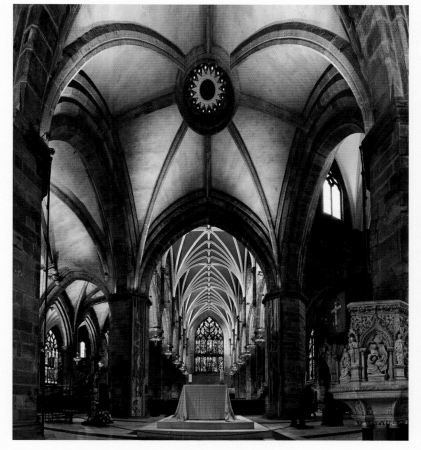

Wide-arched openings reveal the vastness of the interior, which at one time was separated into four sections.

One of the tombs in the cathedral.

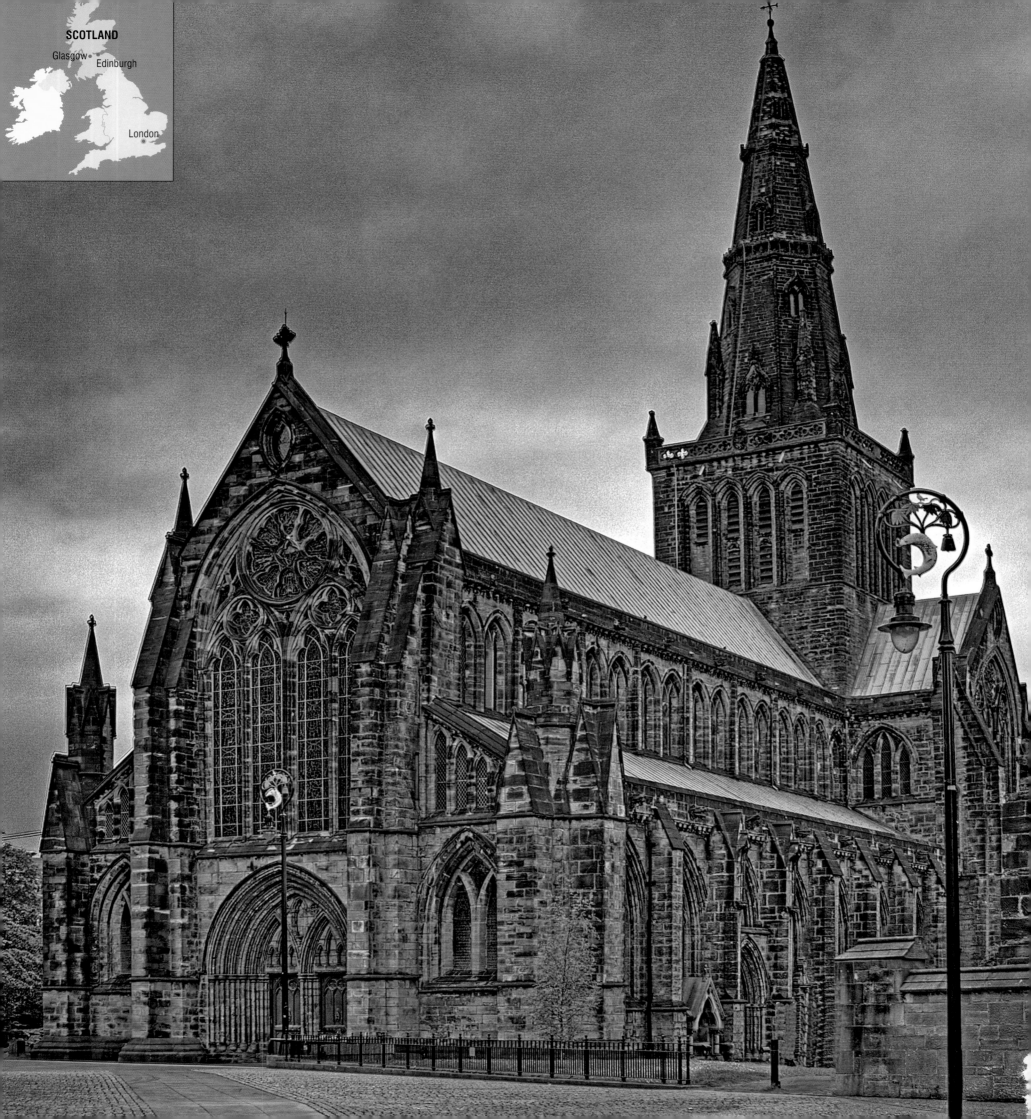

Glasgow Cathedral

Although it is called a cathedral, Glasgow Cathedral has not been the home of a bishopric since 1690. Nonetheless it is the home of the Presbytery of Glasgow, the largest of the 46 presbyteries of the Church of Scotland. It is owned by the Crown and maintained by Historic Scotland, the agency that looks after heritage buildings in the country. It is the largest medieval cathedral in Scotland that has survived the ravages of time intact. Dedicated to St Kentigern (popularly called Mungo, and referred to as the first bishop), who is believed to have established a Christian community in the area around the 7th century, it houses his tomb, and subsequently became a place of pilgrimage. The earliest known record of its existence, however, dates to the time of Bishop John (12th century), when it is said to have been first consecrated. Under Bishop Jocelyn the expanded building was consecrated a second time, and it was under Bishop Bondington (1233–58) that it was finally completed.

Set in the midst of the vibrant industrial city of Glasgow, the cathedral is a refreshing vision of restrained Gothic elegance. A devastating fire in the 12th century, when it was only partially built, motivated a major rebuilding program, begun by Bishop Jocelyn, but modified by successive bishops. Initially, there were to be no aisles, but later the transeptal projection was converted to an aisle. The spacious choir, presbytery, and St Kentigern's shrine chapel are also later additions, not envisaged in the Jocelyn plan. So also is the Blackadder Aisle on the right of the western end. During the Reformation, only the roof was badly damaged by the mobs, and a fortunate survivor was the exquisite rood-screen separating the choir from the nave. The cathedral was for a short while divided into three parts for three different parishes.

NAME	Glasgow Cathedral (High Kirk, St Kentigern's Cathedral, St Mungo's Cathedral)
CONSTRUCTION HISTORY	**12th century** 1st stage of building, consecrated 1136; 2nd stage follows damage by fire; consecrated 1197
	13th century Nave completed; choir, lower church, lower Chapter House built; cathedral complete 2nd 13th century
	1400s Fire; central tower, spire, Chapter House rebuilt
ARCHITECTS	Bishop John, Bishop Jocelyn, Bishop Walter, Bishop William de Bondington
MATERIALS	Stone, timber roof
STYLE	Gothic

The two towers of the cathedral were destroyed in the 19th century and never rebuilt due to lack of funds. Both the great west and east windows are 20th-century additions, as also are most of the stained-glass windows, installed since 1947.

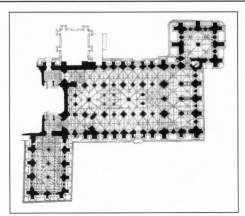

Facing page:
Glasgow Cathedral is a superb example of Scottish Gothic architecture.

The wide and solid nave looking east towards the pulpitum and choir.

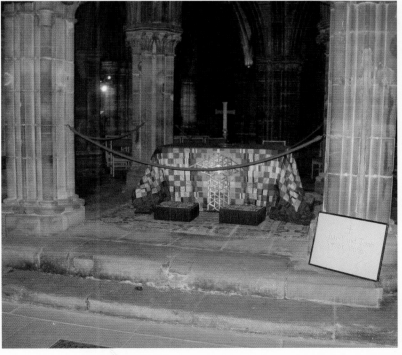

Tomb of St Kentigern (St Mungo).

Santiago de Compostela

· Madrid

SPAIN

Santiago De Compostela Cathedral

After Jerusalem and Rome, Santiago de Compostela is considered the most important place of Christian pilgrimage in medieval times. According to legend, the relics of Christ's apostle, James the Great, were brought to Galicia, Spain, where they were discovered and a shrine built. This was expanded to a cathedral but later burnt down by the armies of the caliph of Cordoba. He left the relics of the Apostle undisturbed but forced his Christian captives to carry the bells and gate of the cathedral to Cordoba. A complete reconstruction of the cathedral began under King Alfonso VI and took 200 years to complete.

One of the most splendid examples of Early Romanesque architecture, the cathedral dominates the Obradoiro plaza in the center of town. A sweeping flight of stairs leads to the original entrance, the Portico de la Gloria, now stepped back behind the magnificent Baroque façade of the 18th century. The highlight of the main doorway is the central column bearing the figure of St James. His statue inside, when touched, marks the completion of the pilgrimage. Beneath the steps lies the vaulted crypt. Comparatively austere inside until the choir bursts forth into the radiating, exuberantly decorated chapels, the vast interior has a barrel-vaulted nave, two side aisles, and a wide transept.

NAME	Santiago de Compostela Cathedral (Catedral de Santiago de Compostela)
ADDRESS	Plaza del Obradoiro, Santiago de Compostela, Galicia, Spain
CONSTRUCTION HISTORY	**9th century** 1st church; later destroyed by Moors
	1075 Construction begun
	11th century Cathedral reconstructed; expanded; consecrated c. 1128
	13th century Main body of cathedral complete
	18th century Baroque façade on the left
COMMISSIONED BY	King Alfonso VI, Bishop Diego Pelaez
ARCHITECTS	Bernard the Elder and Robertus Galperilnus; Fernando Casas y Novoa (façade)
MATERIALS	Granite
STYLE	Early Romanesque; Baroque (façade); Late Gothic (cloisters)

Millions flock to the cathedral every year wearing scallop shells, many choosing to walk, ride, or cycle all the way along the pilgrimage route in order to kiss the statue of the apostle inside. Many make their way on to to Finisterre, the "End of the world'.

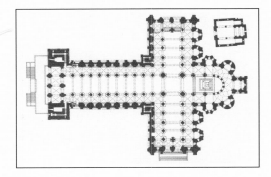

Stone statues line the rooftop over the eastern end.

An interior view of the main body of the cathedral.

Facing page:
The cathedral of Santiago de Compostela is one of the great shrines of Christendom.

Burgos

Madrid

SPAIN

Burgos Cathedral

Burgos was the capital of the united kingdoms of Castile and León for 400 years from the 11th century onwards. It was founded in 884 CE as the frontiers of Christianity were expanding. The wool trade brought it prosperity as did the flow of pilgrims who halted here on their way to the Santiago de Compostela. Perhaps its most familiar association is with Rodrigo Diaz de Vivar, better known as El Cid. This heroic nobleman, who first sold his services to the Moors, switched sides to free his country from Islamic rule, and was elevated to the status of a national hero. He lies buried in the Burgos cathedral, Spain's third largest, built over 300 years. Its diocese was raised to an archbishopric by Pope Gregory XIII in the 16th century at the request of King Philip II.

Designed on the Latin cross plan by architects from France and Germany, it bears great similarities to the traditional French Gothic cathedrals of the time. However, the contact with Islam gave it a veneer of Moorish ornamentation, significantly noticeable in its rich decorative details. The filigree work, a dominant feature of Late Spanish Gothic, which they called 'estilo plateresco' became known as the Plateresque style. Built with the familiar elements of a western façade with triple, arched entrances, surmounted by a rose window, and abutted by two huge but gracefully soaring towers crowned with spires, the footprint of the cathedral is made complex by additions all round. Radiating chapels at different angles and a large bishop's palace to the south add to the complexity. However, its slender pinnacles and lantern tower create a rich silhouette of the cathedral, seen all over the city.

NAME	Cathedral of St Mary (Catedral de Santa Maria e Burgos, Catedral de Burgos)
ADDRESS	Plaza de San Fernando, Burgos, Spain
CONSTRUCTION HISTORY	1221 Construction begun; consecrated 1260
	13th century Choir, transept, cloisters, central part of nave, radiating chapels built; consecrated 1280
	15th century West façade built
	16th century Lantern tower rebuilt after collapse, High Altar built
COMMISSIONED BY	King Ferdinand III and Bishop Mauricio
ARCHITECTS	Enrique (13th century); John of Cologne (15th century)
MATERIALS	Sandstone
STYLE	Gothic, Plateresque

in his *magnum opus* on architecture Banister Fletcher called this "the most poetic of Spanish cathedrals". Its darkest hour was probably during the Spanish Civil War when it became the headquarters of Franco's Fascist government. Fortunately the wealth of its rich ornamentation inside and on the exterior remained untouched.

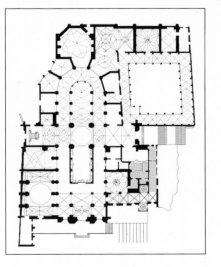

Facing page:
The steel gray spires of Burgos Cathedral are visible from almost anywhere in the city.

Statues, tracery, and gargoyles decorate the cathedral's exterior.

One of the main portals, lined with figures of saints and other biblical figures.

179

Toledo Cathedral

Toledo Cathedral echoes the history of many other cathedrals in Spain. Toledo was the episcopal seat of Visigothic Spain until the Muslim invasion took place. The building was then converted to a mosque, which it remained until King Alfonso VI of León and Castile defeated the Moorish rulers. It was a peaceful transfer of power with the promise to conserve and respect the buildings and customs of the Islamic population. Thus the mosque became a cathedral again. An interesting story recounts the romantic liaison of the queen with the bishop in the absence of the king, who on his return went on a rampage of execution. Not until the caliph was able to pacify him did he stop. In gratitude a statue to the memory of Caliph Walid was placed on a pillar of the mosque-cathedral, where it remains until today.

Almost 300 years in the making resulted in a mix of styles, ranging from pure French Gothic on the exterior to Spanish regional decorative work inside. The grand cathedral has five naves designed to cover the vast area of the mosque, while the courtyard was converted to the cloister. The enthusiastic Archbishop of Toledo was responsible for most of the building work. Regional influences are evident as in the exquisite ironwork in the choir, and the *mudéjar* ceiling of the antechamber of the Chapter House. The interior is filled almost to excess with sumptuous items of religious significance, such as the Crown of our Lady of the Sacrarium and the Cross of Fra Angelico, paintings, and sculptures. Every choir stall is carved with a medieval misericord, depicting a scene from daily life in a comical way. There are more than 20 chapels containing tombs sculpted in fine alabaster or marble.

NAME	Primate Cathedral of St Mary of Toledo (Catedral Primada Santa Maria de Toledo)
ADDRESS	Calle Arco Palacio 2, Toledo, Spain
CONSTRUCTION HISTORY	**578 CE** 1st church on site consecrated
	1226 Cathedral construction begun in reign of Ferdinand III
	13th–14th century 16 Chapels and transept completed
	1493 Building completed; façade, central nave, vaults built
COMMISSIONED BY	King Alfonso VI
ARCHITECTS	Master Martin, Petrus Petri
MATERIALS	White stone from Olihuelas
STYLE	Gothic, Mudéjar

Toledo Cathedral still has services where the Mozarabic Mass, dating to Visigothic times, is celebrated. Many of its decorative items belong to the 18th and 19th centuries.

The High Altar has a polychrome reredos depicting scenes from Christ's life.

The cloisters are on two levels, built on the site of an old Jewish market.

Facing page:
Toledo Cathedral's Gothic spire dominates the view for miles around the city.

León Cathedral

León started as a Roman camp and became the capital of a kingdom in the Middle Ages. Its bishop, first appointed in the 9th century belonged to the Diocese of Toledo. Roman baths originally stood on the site of the cathedral, and were converted to a palace for King Ordono II. Construction of the building began under Bishop Martin Fernandez with money generously given by King Alfonso X, also known as Alfonso the Wise.

Inter-dynastic marriages and cultural connections between France, Germany, and England all had their influences on the development of architecture on the Iberian peninsula but French Gothic was the major stylistic model. Thus, the influence of Reims is particularly noticeable in the layout of the choir and the east end at León. The west end, the transepts, and the delicate interior were modeled on the cathedral of St-Denis, while the one at Ste-Chapelle was a third influence. Therefore, even though León may not have been a royal coronation church or even a pilgrimage site, it stands out for its magnificent use of Gothic elements, albeit with classical restraint. The warm hue of its pale yellow limestone structure not only enhances its architectural and sculptural quality but also the quality of light inside, because of which it is sometimes called the 'House of Light'. León's most attractive feature is the glasswork. Around 180 stained-glass windows date from the 13th to the 20th centuries, illustrating mythical and biblical themes.

NAME	León Cathedral (Catedral de Santa María de Regla de León)
ADDRESS	Plaza de Regla, León, Spain
CONSTRUCTION HISTORY	**1255** Construction begun
	***c.* 14th century** Cathedral complete
	19th century Extensive restoration
COMMISSIONED BY	King Alfonso X
ARCHITECTS	Simón (1261 master builder); Enrique (1277 master builder)
MATERIALS	Golden sandstone
STYLE	Gothic

The cathedral was considered truly complete in the 19th century, when it was also extensively restored. It houses a vast collection of works of sacred art, and was declared a monument of cultural interest in 1844.

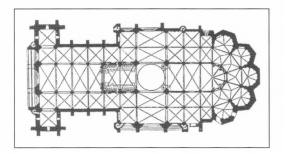

Facing page:
Built in less than 100 years León Cathedral excels in buttressing and vaulting techniques.

A colorful statue of a musician stands out against the golden-hued sandstone structure.

Detail of the main portal with its geometrically patterned door.

SPAIN

Madrid

Seville

Seville Cathedral

Housing the tomb of Christopher Columbus, Seville Cathedral in southern Spain lays claim to being the largest Gothic building in the world. Standing on the banks of the river Guadalquivir, Seville became wealthy as an important shipping center. From here Christopher Columbus and Ferdinand Magellan set sail, and when conquered by the Moors it was filled with Islamic monuments. The cathedral's bell tower, the Giralda, Seville's iconic landmark, was the minaret of a 12th-century mosque. In 1248 Ferdinand III of Castile recaptured the city and made it his home. At first a smaller church was built but later demolished to erect this grand monument to Christianity. It was in part voluntarily paid for by the salaries of church workers who are believed to have said, "Let a church so beautiful and so great be built that those who see it will think we were mad."

Along from the minaret (whose upper part is a Renaissance addition, crowned with Christian symbols), the builders used the spatial structure of the mosque, but added height to it. The square layout has five naves with side chapels. Some columns, the Puerta del Perdon (Gate of Pardon), and the fragrant Patio de los Naranjos (Courtyard of the Orange Trees) are all Moorish originals. The cathedral houses works by the most outstanding painters and sculptors of the time. It was also a setting for the operatic works of Mozart, Bizet, and Rossini. The Capilla Mayor (Main Chapel) has a stunning High Altar (Retablo Mayor), which features the Blessed Virgin Mary in the center, after whom the church is named.

The Giralda, Moorish bell tower, is crowned with a bronze statue symbolizing Faith.

NAME	Cathedral of St Mary of the See (Catedral de Sevilla, Catedral de Santa María de la Sede)
ADDRESS	Avenida de la Constitucion s/n, Seville, Andalusia, Spain
CONSTRUCTION HISTORY	**1402−32** Construction begun; nave built **1506** Cathedral complete and consecrated **16th century** Main dome built, collapses, rebuilt; Capilla Real completed
ARCHITECTS	Pedro Garcia (1421−34); Ysambert (1434); Carlin (1439−49); Juan Norman (1454−1572); Juan de Hoces, Simon of Cologne (crossing tower and dome, 1506)
MATERIALS	Brick (original), masonry, cut stone
STYLE	Gothic

The cathedral's tower dome last collapsed in the late 19th century but rebuilding began almost immediately. DNA tests have being carried out to ascertain the authenticity of Columbus's remains in the tomb ascribed to him.

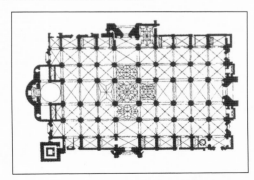

Facing page:
Seville Cathedral stands on the site of a great Almohad mosque of the 12th century.

Cupola over the main sacristy.

SPAIN

Madrid

Cordoba

Cathedral of Cordoba

This most unusual and captivating work of architecture began as a mosque in the 8th century under the enlightened Umayyad dynasty of Cordoba. Its Christian origins however predate the mosque, as the latter itself was built over a Visigothic church which the caliph bought and converted to a mosque. Centuries later, following the Spanish Reconquista, the cathedral was inserted into the structural complex of the Moorish building and is today the seat of the Diocese of Cordoba. The mosque went through several changes under each ruler. One ordered a new minaret, another enlarged it, and the last addition was a connecting raised walkway to the caliph's palace. Elements from a Roman temple and other buildings which had originally stood on the site were reused to fabricate certain sections. Its conversion for use as a cathedral began under the reign of Ferdinand II of Castile. From the building of chapels within the reconsecrated mosque, it evolved into the cathedral under Charles V, and this probably helped it survive the devastating years of the Spanish Inquisition.

Architecturally, the cathedral cannot be viewed in isolation from the mosque, part of which was demolished to build it. Standing centrally, it is part of the sheer magnitude of scale and artistry of the various design elements. Surrounding it, the 850 columns and horseshoe arches of granite, jasper, and marble, the different gates, borrowed either from Islamic or Visigothic precedents, and the mihrab, a marvel of Byzantine ornamentation, all create a visual feast to be savored in the expected stillness of the church. Here too, however, it is an overwhelming experience as one enters the nave. Rich carvings and gilded ornamentation adorn the Baroque choir and Royal Chapel within. The 9th-century minaret at one corner of the entire complex is now the bell tower.

Trees laden with fruit in the adjoining Courtyard of Oranges frame the minaret-bell tower.

NAME	Cathedral of the Assumption of the Virgin (Mezquita-Catedral de Cordoba)
ADDRESS	Calle Torrijos, Cordoba, Spain
CONSTRUCTION HISTORY	**784 CE–12th century** Umayyad mosque built
	13th century Villaviciosa and Royal chapels; consecrated
	1523 Cathedral construction begins inside mosque
	16th century Baroque choir and nave built
COMMISSIONED BY	Abd ar-Rahman I (8th-century mosque); King Ferdinand II (13th-century conversion to church)
ARCHITECTS	Hernán Ruiz family members
MATERIALS	Marble
STYLE	Islamic, Renaissance

It is with a sense of fulfilment that one exits the built up spaces to relax amidst the cool and fragrant courtyard of orange trees, and to marvel at this wonderful confection of religious forms that have earned it the title of a World Heritage Site.

Facing page:
The relative simplicity of the exterior of the Mezquita complex belies the architecturally lavish mosque and cathedral within.

Detail of the entrance doorway leading towards the cathedral.

SPAIN

Barcelona

Madrid

Sagrada Familia

The flamboyantly designed Roman Catholic basilica, Sagrada Familia, is Europe's most unconventional church. A still unfinished project, it was the Catalan architect Antoni Gaudi's obsession for 43 years until his death. He lived on the site like a recluse for 16 years, by which time only one of the 18 towers that he had envisaged had been built. The church was originally commissioned to Francesc de Paula Villar, who resigned after a year. Gaudi took over and completely redesigned the project. After his untimely death in 1926 (he lies buried in the crypt), work continued until the Spanish Civil War 10 years later, when many of the plans and models were destroyed and had to be reformulated. A series of architects have since been engaged. Gaudi was a great believer in hand craftsmanship, a process that made progress painfully slow. Today, computer-aided design technology has helped speed up the work but some say also taken away from its freshness of spirit.

Art Nouveau was adapted by Gaudi in a supremely idiosyncratic style, which he imbued with religious symbolism. There are to be three façades, each with three portals representing Faith, Hope, and Love. Two of them, the Passion Façade (west) and the Nativity Façade (east) are complete. The five-nave basilica is a complex mass of curved lines, minimizing corners and edges. Of the towers, 12 represent the Apostles, four the Evangelists, a short one the Virgin Mary, and the central one, Jesus. The plan of the church is of a Latin cross defined inside by columns and vaulted forms with changing geometric formations, and branching out to support the roof.

NAME	Expiatory Church of the Holy Family (Temple Expiatori de la Sagrada Familia)
ADDRESS	Carrer de Mallorca 401, Barcelona, Spain
CONSTRUCTION HISTORY	**1882** Construction begun
	1884–1900 Crypt and eastern façade built
	1915–1930 Four bell towers complete
	1985 Western façade complete
	2001 Nave vaulting complete
	2010 (expected) Consecration
COMMISSIONED BY	Josep Bocabella
ARCHITECT	Antoni Gaudi
MATERIALS	Masonry
STYLE	Gothic, Art Nouveau

The nave and Glory Façade (south) are still to be built. The expected year of completion is 2026.

Venetian mosaics dominate the tops of the spires, while plant and animal forms in Art Nouveau style are seen on the façade.

Even the sculptural decoration emerges in an organic manner, rich with symbolism.

Facing page:
Construction continues on Gaudi's highly original, contemporary church.

SWEDEN

Stockholm

Lund

Lund Cathedral

The 1000-year-old medieval town of Lund claims to having been the seat of the largest archbishopric in Europe after the present cathedral was built. There had been an earlier church but it is not clear if it was in the same place as today's building. Located at the southern tip of Sweden, Lund was originally a part of the kingdom of Denmark. King Eric I is said to have been granted an archdiocese for all of Scandinavia by the Pope. Bishop Asser was ordained the first bishop in 1104, shortly after which a new cathedral was founded. Around 1164 Sweden acquired its own archbishop. Today Lund is a diocese of the Church of Sweden. The cathedral grew in size following its repair and rebuilding after a major fire in 1234. Nearly all of its religious imagery was done away with during the Reformation, when the influence of the church also diminished. Today's church is the result of restoration works carried out in the late 19th century.

All that remains of the cathedral's original Romanesque form is the crypt and arched gallery of the apse. The former contains a forest of pillars of which the most well-known is that with a man embracing it, supposedly Finn the Giant, who is believed to have built the cathedral. A wealth of local history surrounds the various sarcophagi and graves that lie in the crypt. The choir and altarpiece of the main chapel precede the towers by 500 years; these were added by the Swedish architect restorer Helgo Zettervall in the late 19th century. Entrance to the three-aisled cathedral is through bronze doors sculpted by the 19th-century sculptor Carl Dyfverman. One of the main attractions is the astronomical clock. Though created in 1424, it was kept in storage and brought out only in 1923. It features St Lawrence, patron saint of the cathedral, and the symbols of the Four Evangelists.

Projecting at the east end, the apse is the only survivor of the Romanesque period, along with the crypt.

NAME	Lund Cathedral (Lunds Domkyrka, Saint Lars Cathedral)
ADDRESS	Lund, Skåne län, Sweden
CONSTRUCTION HISTORY	*c.* 1080s Earlier cathedral (correct sp of rarlier)
	1104–45 2nd cathedral built; High Altar and crypt 1123; consecrated 1145
	1234 Major rebuilding occurs after fire
	14th century Gothic choir stalls, altarpiece built
	19th century Rebuilding and restoration
ARCHITECTS	Carl Georg Brunius, Helgo Nikolaus Zettervall, Theodor Wåhlin, Eiler Græbe, Carl-Axel Acking, and others (19th/20th century)
MATERIALS	Sandstone, granite
STYLE	Romanesque

Sacred music concerts are regularly held in the cathedral and it is also used as a place where academic degrees are conferred.

The central panel of the lavish altarpiece.

Facing page:
Carved out of granite blocks undisguised by ornamentation, Lund Cathedral has an awesome exterior.

SWEDEN

Uppsala

Stockholm

Uppsala Cathedral

Sweden was Christianized around 1000 CE and before Uppsala was made the archdiocese of the country in 1164, Gamla, or Old Uppsala, was the ecclesiastical center, where a small stone church stood. Construction of the present cathedral began when Uppsala superseded Gamla, a neglected town after the ruling family moved to Stockholm. It was dedicated to St Eric, Sweden's medieval king and patron saint, who propogated Christianity. He had been murdered by the Danes, and buried in Uppsala, which was his capital. The saints Lawrence and Olaf, also highly revered by the Swedes, share the title of the cathedral. It separated from the Roman Catholic church after the Reformation to follow the Lutheran branch of Christianity.

Predominantly Gothic in appearance, the cathedral was originally based on English models. In the 13th century the French architect Etienne de Bonneuil was commissioned and built the graceful Gothic spires. They were later recapped in a Baroque style after fire partly damaged them in 1702. The interior too is unmistakably Gothic with clusters of slim columns interspersed with long arched openings holding up the vaulted nave. Just as the red brick exterior warmly glows against the stark white snowy landscape in winter, the interior of the cathedral too has an inviting ambience. Light from the windows and clerestories fills the corners, illuminating the painted nave ceiling and walls around the main altar and ambulatory. The relics of St Eric lie in a golden coffin in one of the chapels off the nave. Members of the royal family, the botanist Carolus Linnaeus, philosopher Emanuel Swedenborg, ecclesiastical figures, and Nobel Prize winner Dag Hammarskjöld are among those that are honored by memorials or tombs inside.

The red brick façade elegantly offsets the striking stone portal and rose window above it.

NAME	Cathedral of Ss Lawrence, Erik, and Olaf (Uppsala Domkyrka)
ADDRESS	Domkyrkoplan 2, Uppsala, Sweden
CONSTRUCTION HISTORY	**1287–1435** Cathedral built and consecrated
	18th century Fire; towers rebuilt; spires built
	end 19th century Restoration
COMMISSIONED BY	Archbishop of Gamma Uppsala
ARCHITECTS	Etienne de Bonneuil, Carl Hårleman (restoration mid 18th century); Helgo Zettervall (restoration 19th/20th century)
MATERIALS	Brick
STYLE	Renaissance, Baroque, Gothic Revival

Successive restorations introduced different styles over the years but the trend is to recover as much of the cathedral's medieval character as possible. No longer a state church since 2000, its liberal orientation now allows women to be ordained as priests.

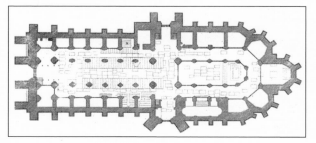

Facing page:
Uppsala Cathedral's contrasting gray and red exterior is highlighted against the winter landscape.

Tombstone of the famous botanist Carolus Linnaeus.

Geneva Cathedral

Geneva Cathedral is also referred to as the Temple of St Peter, and dates to Roman times when a large Christian community must have resided here. The fascinating archaeological site, which lies beneath the building bears the remains of two 4th-century Christian shrines that existed here many centuries before the cathedral which we see today was built. There is also evidence of three earlier churches and an 11th-century crypt which must have been part of the first Romanesque cathedral that preceded this one. Previously affiliated to the Roman Catholic church it is now a member of the Swiss Reformed Church. The cathedral stands on a high point in Old Geneva and is best known as the place where John Calvin, the Protestant reformer preached, marking the turning point of the church's affiliation around 1536. His wooden chair is one of the most important exhibits of the church.

There is no single style in the architectural vocabulary of the church as it underwent periodic changes. Most of all, it was shorn of its Roman Catholic adornments following the Reformation and so, apart from the stained-glass windows, little remains of its original artefacts. An important architectural change was the superimposing of the original façade with a Neo-Classical one. In fact, the original porch now lies behind the row of columns and new portal that mark the entrance. The two towers also exhibit dissimilarity in that the later 19th-century one rises high above the other in a bright green hue. In any case, the original two towers were never completed. Inside, however, the nave, with its Romanesque columns and capitals still remain. The 14th-century Chapel of the Maccabees was remodeled in the 19th / 20th centuries in an attractive High Gothic mode. The same style distinguishes the choir stalls which are remnants from the destroyed Chapelle des Florentins.

NAME	Cathedral of St Peter (Cathédral St-Pierre)
ADDRESS	Cours St-Oierre 6, 1204 Geneva, Switzerland
CONSTRUCTION HISTORY	**1000** Earlier cathedral (Romanesque)
	1160–1310 Present cathedral built
	1397 Chapelle of the Maccabees
	15th century Fire destroys a tower; choir stalls built
	c. **1750** New Neo-Classical façade built
MATERIALS	Stone
STYLE	Romanesque, Gothic, Neo-Classical

A chapel dedicated to the Duc of Rohan, leader of the French Protestants in the reign of Louis XIII was added in 1889. The modern organ is only about 50 years old. The last renovations were completed in the late 1970s.

Steps leading to the pulpit, surmounted by a carved wooden canopy.

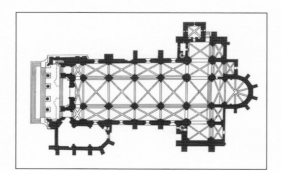

Facing page:
Geneva Cathedral is a complex ensemble of architecturally different elements.

Calvin's chair, a prized possession of the cathedral.

SWITZERLAND

Berne

Lausanne

Lausanne Cathedral

The Protestant cathedral of Lausanne is one of the oldest Gothic cathedrals outside France, after Canterbury. Situated on Lake Geneva, it mostly borrowed its aesthetics from France but also displayed a great affinity to England's Canterbury Cathedral. It was built in stages (the first two architects are unknown), with the main section begun by Jean de Cotereel. Both the emperor Rudolph of Habsburg and Pope Gregory X consecrated it as a place of Christian worship. It was dedicated to the Virgin Mary, whose statue in gold, referred to as the Golden Virgin in the Middle Ages attracted large crowds of pilgrims. Unfortunately the statue was burnt down to make coins during the Reformation of the 16th century.

Bearing all the traditional Gothic elements—towers and spires, long arched openings, and a vaulted nave that is the height of elegance in its simplicity—the cathedral has some remarkable features. First, the existence of an ambulatory is unusual for a cathedral of such an early date in the Gothic style. It is defined by pillars surmounted by arches on three levels. Many columns in the transept area still bear traces of paint from medieval times. The giant south rose window is another outstanding element, with its imagery displaying the medieval view of cosmology. So striking a work of art was it that the great French architect, Villard de Honnecourt, copied it on paper for future reference. Much of the original interior decoration was stripped during the Reformation years but the entrance, through the Montfalcon Portal on the west, retains its statuary of bishops, saints, and other figures.

Embedded in the front stone walls is the splendid Montfalcon Portal.

NAME	Cathedral of Our Lady of Lausanne (Cathédrale Notre-Dame de Lausanne)
ADDRESS	Place de la Cathédrale, Lausanne,, Switzerland
CONSTRUCTION HISTORY	*c.* **1170** Construction begun on 1st stage
	1190–1215 2nd stage completed
	1215 onwards 3rd stage building leading to present cathedral
	1275 Cathedral consecrated
ARCHITECTS	Jean de Cotereel; Eugène Viollet-le-Duc (19th century)
MATERIALS	Stone
STYLE	Gothic

Today the cathedral is the last survivor of an age-old Swiss tradition where the night watchmen called out on the hour to reassure everyone that the city was safe; every night the call is still made from 10pm to 2am. After Viollet-le-Duc's masterful restoration in the 19th century, the cathedral's latest face-lift was given in 2007.

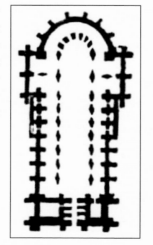

Facing page:
Lausanne Cathedral is famous for its tower from which the nightwatchman makes his hourly announcement.

Patterned with clear geometric outlines, the front rose window is a stunning work of art.

Zurich

Berne

SWITZERLAND

Grossmunster

The most prominent landmark in Zurich, Grossmünster was a monastery church, whose legendary beginnings attribute it to Charlemagne. The great king is reputed to have been passing by the graves of three early Christian martyrs, Felix, Regula, and Exuperantius, when his horse stopped. The three, it is said, were to be executed when they had fled but were caught by the governor and subjected to terrible torture since they would not recant their faith. Eventually, though severely burnt, they climbed atop a hill, dug their own graves and buried themselves. It is on this site that the Charlemagne ordered the cathedral to be built in their names; they are the patron saints of Zurich, whose images have since been used on official seals and coins. Renovations continued until the time of the Reformation, when a contemporary of Martin Luther, Huldrych Zwingli, a radical reformist, advocated religious freedom and abolition of all religious iconography. He died in a conflict between Roman Catholics and Protestants but his was a defining era in the history of the church, transforming Zurich into a major Protestant religious center.

Romanesque in its architecture, which is all the more apparent since the decorative trappings were removed, the cathedral retains a few of its early carvings and frescoes, though faded. The north portal, a side chapel, as also the small undercroft chapel and crypt remind one of its origins. Charlemagne's discovery of the martyrs' graves is picturised on some of the capitals, along with battle scenes. The crypt also contains a 15th-century statue of the emperor, which once stood atop the south tower — the tower now has a replica. Most of the decorative aspects of the cathedral are however, modern.

NAME	Cathedral of Sts Felix, Regula, and Exuperantius (Great Minster)
ADDRESS	Grossmünsterplatz, Zurich, Switzerland
CONSTRUCTION HISTORY	**1090–1230** Cathedral built
COMMISSIONED BY	Emperor Charlemagne
MATERIALS	Stone
STYLE	Romanesque

The twin towers of the cathedral, originally wooden, were destroyed in a fire in 1781. They have since been rebuilt in Gothic style. The stained-glass windows—three being the work of Augusto Giacometti—and ornate bronze doors on both north and south portals also date to the 20th century. The cloister houses a museum on the Reformation.

Facing page:
Grossmünster is one of Zurich's three main churches.

Stunning in their imagery the stained-glass windows are also sculpturesque in form.

Charlemagne sits at the southern tower—the original statue is kept in the crypt.

Berne Cathedral

The Gothic cathedral of Berne was built on the site of two previous churches when the 10th-century city started to become wealthy and important in the 15th century. The preceding church continued to be used for services and was only demolished when the choir of the new one was covered with a simple roof and stained-glass windows had been installed. Matthaus Ensinger, the architect from Strasbourg who had already built three other cathedrals, was appointed. After him a number of master masons supervised the building as the basic structure of the cathedral expanded. Following completion of the central nave, work stopped for almost three centuries. During this period, the church also changed from Roman Catholic to Protestant affiliation, and as was the case with other such institutions during the height of the Reformation movement, it was subject to Protestant iconoclasm. Only when the bell tower was built was the cathedral finally recognized as complete.

The entrance portal contains perhaps the most arresting feature of the entire cathedral, a wood and stone portrayal of *The Last Judgment*. Surprisingly this elaborate work of Gothic art was left untouched by the iconoclastic crowds. So too were the roof bosses of Christ, the Virgin Mary, and saints, and the carved choir stalls. Other changes have, however, occurred, such as in the side chapels, which became starker, with pews replacing the erstwhile decorative altars. Many of the sculptures from here were used as fillings for the cathedral's terrace, which overlooks the river Aare. The original nave, described as "lacy Gothic" was raised in hieght and vaulting begun at the same time as the tower was begun. When complete, it was reputed to be the highest church in Switzerland with its new steeple (1893).

NAME	Cathedral of St Vincent (Bern Münster)
ADDRESS	Münsterplatz, 3011 Bern, Switzerland
CONSTRUCTION HISTORY	**12th–13th centuries** 1st and 2nd churches on site
	1421 Present cathedral begun; main portal and pulpit built 15th century
	1575 Central nave completed
	1893 Bell tower and spire built; church complete
COMMISSIONED BY	City of Berne
ARCHITECTS	Matthäus Ensinger, Stefan Hurder, Niklaus Birenvogt, Erhard Küng, Peter Pfister, Daniel Heintz (master masons)
MATERIALS	Local sandstone
STYLE	Gothic

The cathedral's tower provides wonderful views of the Alps and other mountains. There is also, surprisingly, an apartment almost halfway up, which was the warden's residence for years, and is now an office. The terrace, too, which used to be a graveyard in the 15th century, is now an open plaza, beautifully landscaped, and a popular place for visitors.

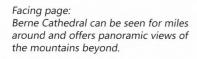

Facing page:
Berne Cathedral can be seen for miles around and offers panoramic views of the mountains beyond.

The Last Judgment *is elaborately portrayed on the richly embellished entrance portal.*

Some of the most beautiful stained-glass windows in the world are found in this cathedral.

Kiev

UKRAINE

St Sophia Cathedral

UNESCO World Heritage Site

The name St Sophia given to Ukraine's spectacular cathedral is derived from the 6th-century Hagia Sophia of Constantinople, the splendid cathedral of Orthodox Christendom. Some believe that the cathedral was modeled on the 13-domed St Sophia of Novgorod. The latter had been built around the same time as the Ukraine cathedral, by Yaroslav I in gratitude for having been made king. Kiev, the capital of the newly founded (1990s) country of Ukraine was also the capital of the Vikings in the 9th century. Their kingdom then was called Kievan Rus and it was under their successors, the Ruriks, that Christianity came to the country. The Eastern Roman or Orthodox church is governed by autonomous patriarchs; the principal patriarch was for long based in Constantinople. In style and religious imagery it is also therefore based on the rich religious iconography of the Byzantine tradition. St Sophia, which took two decades to complete became a model for churches in the eastern Slavic states.

After it was badly mutilated by Genghiz Khan's hordes in the 13th century the cathedral fell into disrepair, and it was centuries later that restoration of the old building began. From its original 12 hemispherical domes placed around a central more heavily gilded one, there were now 20. The profusion of domes and clusters of semi-circular apses grouped around the building is the classic familiar form of most Russian Orthodox churches today, as is the Greek cross plan, which provides the footprint for this cathedral as well. The interior has two galleries, the upper one connected to the tsar's residence and was used for his family, while the lower one was for commoners. Mosaics and frescoes are in abundance, some depicting secular themes such as the games held in the Hippodrome in Constantinople.

NAME	St Sophia's Cathedral
ADDRESS	Kiev, Ukraine
CONSTRUCTION HISTORY	*c.* **1037–1050s** Original cathedral built
	17th–18th century Restoration and rebuilding of present cathedral
COMMISSIONED BY	Yaroslav I the Wise
ARCHITECTS	Octaviano Mancini, Hetman Ivan Mazepa (17th-18th century)
MATERIALS	Brick, plaster
STYLE	Byzantine, Ukranian Baroque

After the Russian Revolution the cathedral faced replacement by a park, but was fortunately saved and designated an architectural and historical museum. No religious services are allowed inside.

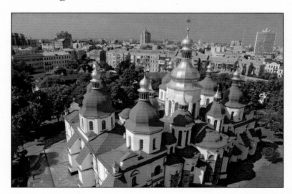

Facing page:
The many domed basilica of St Sophia became a model for churches in the eastern Slavic countries.

A statue of one of the legendary heroes in Ukraine's history stands in front of the cathedral.

Stucco work ornaments the walls.

St Louis Cathedral

St Louis Cathedral has a dramatic history but despite the damage it has suffered time and again, it bears the distinction of being the oldest continuously used Roman Catholic cathedral in America. The present building is largely a result of the expansion and rebuilding that took place of the brick and timber church of the 1720s when it was destroyed by the great fire of 1788. Before that there existed yet another crude wooden structure servicing the needs of the first settlers in the colony; this was destroyed by a hurricane. The cathedral occupies a coveted site facing the Mississippi River and bordered by historic buildings. It was severely damaged in 1909 when a bomb blew up inside it, and again in 1915 by a devastating hurricane. The next year, part of the foundation collapsed. Renovation and the decision to enlarge it then resulted in the cathedral that we see today in the French Quarter of the city.

Built in brick taken from the original town cemetery and plastered, its western façade ends in two towers on either side with conical black spires in sharp contrast to the stuccoed white exterior. The main tower over the crossing soars above these two and creates a classic church silhouette. During expansion all but the side walls and lower portions of the towers were demolished. Later, even the central tower collapsed, so what is seen today retains little of its Spanish colonial original form. The vaulted nave inside has a painted ceiling and an open gallery on the upper level that rests on smooth circular columns.

In the cloister of the cathedral.

NAME	St Louis Cathedral (Basilica of St Louis, King of France)
ADDRESS	615 Pere Antoine Alley, New Orleans, Louisiana, USA
CONSTRUCTION HISTORY	**1718** 1st church built on site
	1725–27 2nd church built on site
	1788 / 89 Fire destroys church; cornerstone laid of present church; raised to rank of cathedral in 1793
	1794 Cathedral completed
	1845–51 Expansion and rebuilding
ARCHITECT	JNB de Pouilly
MATERIALS	Brick
STYLE	Renaissance, Spanish Colonial

The cathedral was designated a minor basilica by Pope Paul VI in 1964, and blessed by Pope John Paul's visit in 1987. In the hurricane prone region where it stands, it was last hammered by Hurricane Katrina, which tore a hole in the roof that damaged the organ. Extensive restoration took place in 2004.

Facing page:
The elegant design of St Louis Cathedral complements the colonial architecture of its surroundings.

A beautiful ceiling fresco of Jesus with his disciples under the protection of the Father.

USA

New York

Washington DC

St Patrick's Cathedral

The introduction to *St Patrick's Cathedral: A Centennial History* states: "In the Old World, for well over a thousand years the center of a city was thought to be wherever its Cathedral stood." However, when Archbishop Hughes proposed the building of the new St Patrick's where it now stands he was ridiculed for siting it in a near wilderness and his plan referred to as Hughes' Folly. Today, the cathedral site is the heart of Manhattan, beside the Rockefeller Center, a testimony to the Roman Catholic bishop's foresight and persistence. He was also responsible for expanding the old St Patrick's. Funds for the new cathedral were raised by organizing a fair. Work came to a halt during the Civil War in 1865 but when resumed, continued into the 20th century, with the Lady Chapel and other significant additions.

The marble-covered brick building has had several superb designers and craftsmen work on it. Artists from Chartres, Birmingham, and Boston have contributed to the stained-glass windows; Tiffany & Co designed the St Michael and St Louis altars, while the St Elizabeth altar was the work of Paolo Medici of Rome; the Pietà, three times larger than Michelangelo's famous sculpture, was made by Araldo Perugi. Extensive renovations in the 20th century restored both the interior and magnificent Gothic exterior, replacing much of the roof, relocating the baptistery, and installing shrines in honor of American saints.

NAME	St Patrick's Cathedral
ADDRESS	Fifth Avenue and 50th St, New York City, NY 110025, USA
CONSTRUCTION HISTORY	**18th century** St Peter's Church built
	1809 Cornerstone laid of (Old) St Patrick's Cathedral; destroyed by fire in 1866
	1858 Cornerstone laid of new St Patrick's Cathedral; opened 1879
	1888 Spires completed
	1911 Cathedral consecrated
	1927 Renovation program begun; enlargement and rebuilding
COMMISSIONED BY	Archbishop John Hughes
ARCHITECT	James Renwick, Jr
MATERIALS	Brick, marble facing, slate (roof)
STYLE	Gothic Revival

The Requiem Masses of famous Americans have been said here: Babe Ruth, Robert Kennedy, Andy Warhol, and firefighters who died in the disaster of 2001. The tombs of past archbishops rest in the crypt behind the High Altar, above which hang their *galeros* (ceremonial hats).

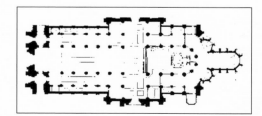

Facing page:
St Patrick's is the largest Roman Catholic cathedral in the United States.

Detail of the façade portal.

Gracefully encased within an arch, the rose window exemplifies stonecarving skills.

Cathedral of St John the Divine

The cathedral of the Episcopal Diocese of New York, St John the Divine, will be among the largest churches in the world when finished. Covering an area of 87,600 sq ft (8000 sq m), it was designed more than 100 years ago through an open competition. The foundations had to be laid at an extraordinary depth of 72 ft (22 m) where the first layers of bedrock were found. The premature death of the principal designer brought a halt to the work. A further hiatus occurred when World War II broke out. More than 35 years later, Bishop Paul Moore revived construction, using the project to train local youth in stonemasonry. The cathedral remains incomplete, despite its active role in the community.

The original design envisaged a Romanesque plan and architecture. However, when the architect of this scheme died his successor gave it a Gothic remodeling after the classical style of northern France, which is its primary image today. Certain sections however, retain their original style, such as the Romanesque crossing and dome, Norman and Byzantine chapels, and Roman arches and columns separating the High Altar and ambulatory. The design of seven chapels represents each of the seven most prominent ethnic groups to have migrated to America in 1892. The Great West Rose Window has been designed as a sort of mandala, based on a complicated geometric plan and made up of 10,000 pieces of colored glass.

NAME	Cathedral Church of St John the Divine
ADDRESS	1047 Amsterdam Avenue, New York, NY 10025, USA
CONSTRUCTION HISTORY	**1888–92** Designed and cornerstone laid
	1911 Plan changed to Gothic; choir and crossing opened
	1941 Cathedral opened; work halted by World War II
	1978 Construction resumed
	1997 Western façade completed
COMMISSIONED BY	Rt Rev Horatio Potter, Bishop of New York
ARCHITECTS	George Lewis Heins and C Grant LaFarge (original design); Ralph Adams Cram (nave and Gothic remodeling); John Thomas Doran
MATERIALS	Granite, Guastavino tiles (dome); limestone (upper part of south tower)
STYLE	Gothic Revival; Romanesque (crossing); Norman and Byzantine (chapels)

A massive restoration program was begun in 2007. Two quaint annual services are held here: Blessing of the Animals, which allows entry to pets of all sizes; and Blessing of the Bikes, which draws earnest, helmeted bikers with their machines inside.

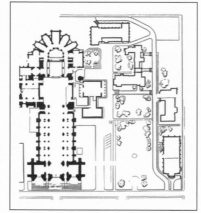

The ornate rose window and entrance portal.

Altar area of the cathedral.

Facing page:
The incomplete St John the Divine is nevertheless a vital part of New York life.

Washington National Cathedral

Although land had been set aside for a "great church for national purposes" when Washington DC was planned in 1792, it was not until 1893 that Congress gave the go-ahead to the Episcopal Cathedral Foundation to build the cathedral. A new site on Mount St Alban was chosen as the earlier one had since been occupied by the National Portrait Gallery. President Roosevelt laid the foundation stone, and within five years, the Bethlehem Chapel was opened for services. The money for its building and maintenance came from private sources and continues to do so. The cathedral took 83 years to complete.

In style, the building stands up magnificently to the great Gothic masterpieces of Europe: flying buttresses, exquisite stained glass, high vaulted naves, a soaring bell tower. The crypt chapels have greater affinity to the Norman, Romanesque, and intermediary styles preceding the Gothic. There are many 'intentional' flaws, in line with a medieval custom that eschews absolute perfection in the belief that only God can be perfect. Thus, there are certain asymmetries, such as the nave slightly tilting off axis as it approaches the transept crossing. Among the art pieces of interest is the Space Window, which has a piece of moon rock embedded in it.

NAME	Cathedral Church of St Peter and St Paul (National Cathedral)
ADDRESS	3101 Wisconsin Avenue NW, Washington, DC, USA
CONSTRUCTION HISTORY	**1907** Construction begun
	1912 Cathedral consecrated; Bethlehem Chapel opened
	1977 West rose window dedicated
	1990 Cathedral complete
COMMISSIONED BY	United States Congress / Protestant Episcopal Cathedral Foundation
ARCHITECTS	George Frederick Bodley; Frederick Law Olmsted, Jr (landscape); Henry Vaughan; Philip Hubert Frohman (post World War I)
MATERIALS	Gray Indiana limestone, concrete, steel
STYLE	Neo-Gothic

Numerous famous names are associated with the cathedral. Martin Luther King gave his last Sunday sermon here; Helen Keller and President Woodrow Wilson are among those buried inside; state funerals for presidents Eisenhower and Reagan have been held here. In keeping with its spirit of being a national cathedral, it has been temporary home of other religious communities too, such as the Jewish and Eastern Orthodox from time to time.

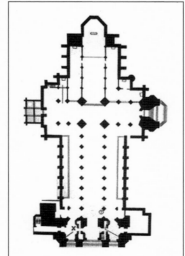

Facing page:
Washington National Cathedral's Gothic architecture is a magnificent tribute to its national status.

View of the sanctuary.

Section of the splendid display of stained-glass windows in the cathedral.

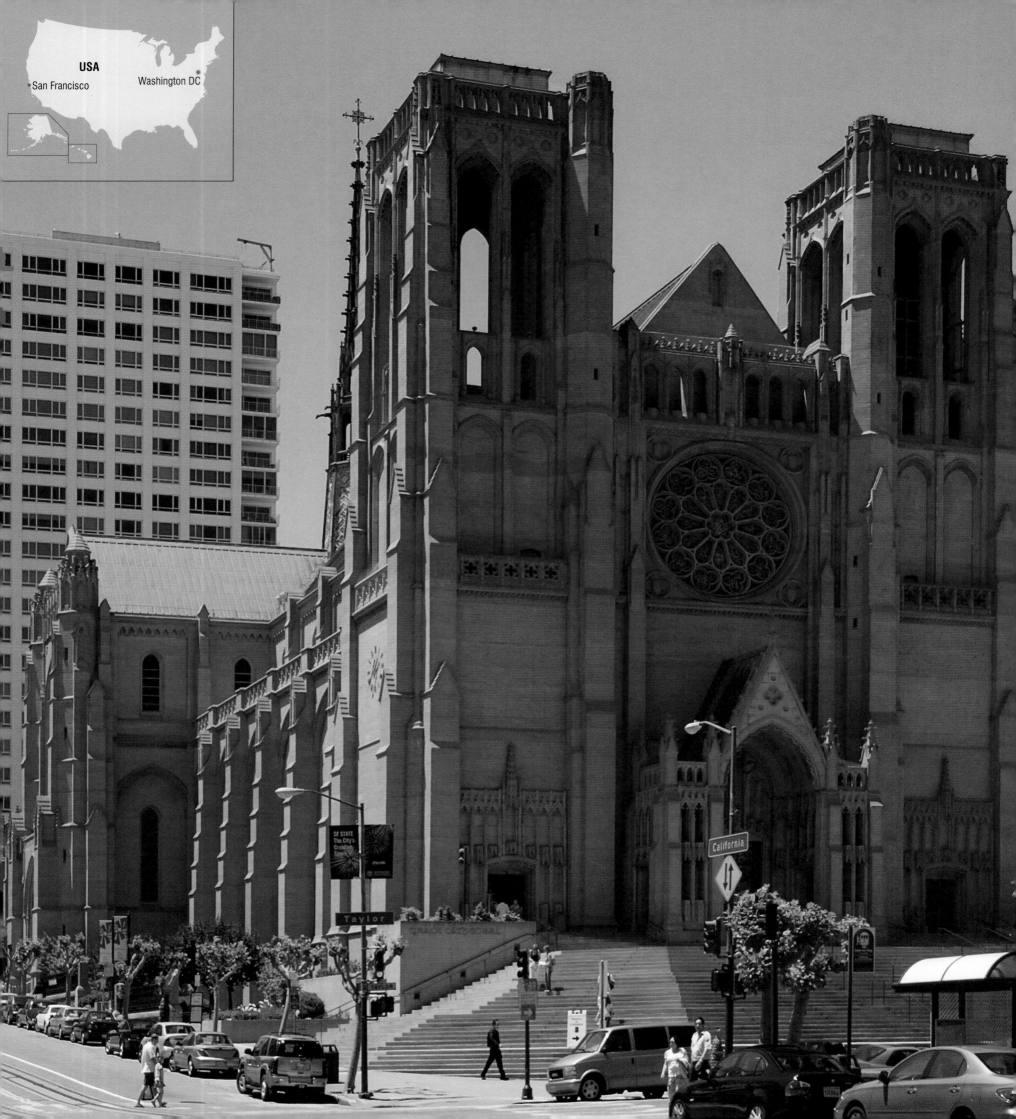

Grace Cathedral

Standing on an elevated spot in San Francisco, where the first small chapel was built during the Gold Rush years, Grace Cathedral is the last of several rebuildings. When the third church, grandest of them all and called Grace Cathedral, was burnt down following the devastating earthquake of 1906, a banker generously donated his Nob Hill property for a new building. This took 36 years to build and was inspired by the architecture of Notre-Dame in Paris. It is the cathedral of the Episcopalian Diocese of California and house of worship for a vibrant resident community.

Inspired by the Sainte-Chapelle Cathedral in France, the first unit of Grace Cathedral to be built was the Grace Chapel. All the features inside it go back either to medieval times or later English Gothic or Italian Renaissance, such as the painting of *Mother and Child*. Other influences from cathedrals in Europe, apart from Paris's Notre-Dame are apparent. Of the two labyrinths, the one inside on a large rug borrows from the stone original at Chartres; the exquisite bronze Doors of Paradise at the east end are replicas of Ghiberti's in the Florence cathedral's baptistery. A French artist from Chartres designed the 24 faceted windows featuring human endeavor, with images of John Glenn, Robert Frost, and others. A triptych altarpiece symbolizes the fight against AIDS, and an image of St Francis of Assisi recalls San Francisco's early days when the Franciscans first landed in California, and established the first diocese.

NAME	Grace Cathedral
ADDRESS	1100 California St, San Francisco, CA 94108, USA
CONSTRUCTION HISTORY	**1849** 1st chapel (Grace Church) built; rebuilt twice and called Grace Cathedral
	1906 Destroyed by an earthquake
	1928–64 Present cathedral built and consecrated
COMMISSIONED BY	Diocese of California
ARCHITECT	Lewis P Hobart
MATERIALS	Reinforced concrete, steel
STYLE	Neo-Gothic

This 20th-century church, enriched by its Neo-Gothic architecture and exquisite art collection takes its place in popular culture having been featured in songs and films. It may be medieval in appearance, but is fitted with the latest technology, especially in view of the fragile earthquake prone zone in which it stands.

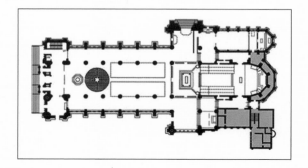

Facing page:
Grace Cathedral is the spiritual center of San Francisco's Episcopalian community.

The famous replica of Ghiberti's bronze Doors of Paradise.

Christ depicted in contemporary imagery in stained glass.

USA

Washington DC

Garden Grove

Crystal Cathedral

When the Rev Robert Schuller and his wife arrived in Garden Grove, California, in 1955 to spread the Christian faith under the patronage of the Reformed Church in America, their first stop was at a drive-in theater. Here they initially held weekly services. It was an unusual location, being open, but precisely because of this, gained in popularity as it was easily accessible to everyone. Schuller spread the message of hope, rather than sin and atonement, and the large attendance was sufficient motivation to plan on a more permanent building. The Californian architect Richard Neutra was asked to design a church that would have both closed and openable spaces. In the meantime Schuller had begun telecasting his program and this gave an extraordinary thrust to his popularity. A larger church became necessary, which was then given to the famed Philip Johnson to design.

"Make it all glass!" were the guidelines given to Johnson. Richard Neutra's design, too, had had an abundance of the see-through material. Johnson, acclaimed for his engineering and architectural skills, designed an all-glass structure supported on a steel frame—the church has 10,000 windows. Amazingly, it is not air-conditioned and relies on natural air currents entering through staggered windows, and controlled thermostatically. To facilitate the system, the new design incorporated two tall doors from Neutra's earlier building. The all-glass design is also remarkable in that it can withstand earthquakes of magnitude 8.0. The four-pointed star plan has free-standing balconies at three points and the chancel in the fourth.

NAME	Crystal Cathedral
ADDRESS	12141 Lewis St, Garden Grove, CA 92840, USA
CONSTRUCTION HISTORY	**1962** 1st church built
	1978 Present cathedral begun and consecrated
	1980 Cathedral built and consecrated
	1990 Cathedral tower consecrated
COMMISSIONED BY	Reverend Robert H Schuller
ARCHITECTS	Richard Neutra (1st church); Philip Johnson with John Burgee (present cathedral)
MATERIALS	Steel and glass, marble chancel
STYLE	Modern

This megachurch can seat 3000 and is not strictly a cathedral in the sense of being the official seat of a bishop. Originally titled Garden Grove Community Church, it was dubbed a cathedral on its dedication in 1980. Since the 1990s it has been adorned with various modern statues and also endowed with its iconic bell.

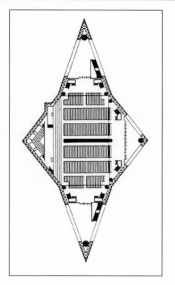

Facing page:
Crystal Cathedral's megastructure is a far cry from its original home in a drive-in theater.

The all-glass cathedral is technically designed to withstand earthquake damage.

A view of the organs against the shimmering glass backdrop.

USA

Washington DC

Los Angeles

Los Angeles Cathedral

The 11-story Cathedral of Our Lady of the Angels in Los Angeles was the first Roman Catholic cathedral to be built in the western United States in 30 years. It was built to replace the earlier St Vibiana's, which had been severely damaged during an earthquake. This former cathedral housed the relics of the 3rd-century martyr, St Vibiana, which had been brought to Los Angeles from Rome in 1854. While many argued that the old historic structure should be repaired for reuse, the city ultimately sold the property to a developer, who converted the old cathedral to a performance center. The archdiocese then bought a large new site, and with generous funding coming in from various quarters, the design was commissioned to a famous Spanish architect. The title of the cathedral had already been approved by the Pope in 1945 when earlier plans had been made to reconstruct St Vibiana's.

The cathedral serves a multi-cultural population so the idea was to give it an eclectic image. 'Light' and 'Journey', as in pilgrimage towards finding the Kingdom of God, were the unifying themes. Entering through monumental bronze doors on the south side, a contemporary statue of the Virgin Mary, depicted as a working woman with a mix of ethnic features, welcomes the visitor. The doors are decorated with cultural and symbolic motifs instead of the usual biblical themes. There are virtually no right angles and earthquake safeguards have been installed in the geometrically complex structure. While the huge space inside can accommodate 3000 persons, the crypt below, which is the last resting place of St Vibiana, past bishops, and famous people such as Gregory Peck, has space for 6000 burials.

Statue of the Virgin Mary depicted as a working woman.

NAME	Cathedral of Our Lady of the Angels (Los Angeles Cathedral)
ADDRESS	555 West Temple St, Los Angeles, CA 90012, USA
CONSTRUCTION HISTORY	**1876** Cathedral of St Vibiana built; damaged in earthquake of 1994
	1998–2002 Present cathedral built and consecrated
COMMISSIONED BY	Cardinal Mahony/City of Los Angeles
ARCHITECTS	Rafael Moneo; Robert Graham (bronze doors)
MATERIALS	Concrete, alabaster windows
STYLE	Modern, Post Modern

The final cost of the cathedral was close to $200 million dollars, because of which many critics dubbed it the "Taj Mahony". This prize-winning work of architecture today celebrates Mass in 42 different languages and attracts countless pilgrims.

Facing page:
The contemporary design of the cathedral won its architect a prestigious architecture award.

A detail from John Nava's tapestry of the communion of saints.

WALES
St David's   London

St David's Cathedral

St David's is one of the oldest cathedrals in Britain, standing on the site of a 6th-century monastery that was established by the Celtic monk Dewi (translated as David in Norman). It is located in an isolated part of the Pembrokeshire peninsula jutting out into the Atlantic Ocean. Known for his wisdom, learning, and extreme asceticism David was honored as the patron saint of Wales when he died and the monastic church was soon raised to a cathedral and a place of pilgrimage. In 1115 King Henry I appointed Bernard as the first Norman archbishop, who dedicated a new cathedral in 1131. This was later rebuilt towards the close of the century. The 14th-century Bishop Henry Gower was one of the principal figures to have influenced the form of the cathedral until it was greatly restored and remodeled between the 19th and 21st centuries.

Built of the local purple hued Cambrian sandstone in a Norman style, it is relatively austere on the exterior. Inside, looking down the nave, most striking is the tilt of the floor and veering of the arcades outwards, which has been ascribed to the sloping and marshy site, as well as to an earthquake in 1248. The ceiling above, as well as the choir, with its collection of decorated misericords, testify to the ingenuity of woodcraftsmen of the era. The Shrine of St David was robbed of its relics during the Reformation. These are now believed to lie in the Holy Trinity Chapel built by Bishop Vaughn. Tombs and figures of various saints, priests, and knights fill the interior. There is also a stained-glass image of St David in the St Thomas Becket Chapel.

Considerably weathered by time, the Norman fortress-like cathedral continues to be an active place of worship.

NAME	St David's Cathedral
ADDRESS	Cathedral Close, St David's, Pembrokeshire, Wales, UK
CONSTRUCTION HISTORY	**6th century** Monastery church; raised to cathedral
	1131 New cathedral dedicated; rebuilt 1180–82
	13th century Collapse of new tower, repaired; Chapel of St Thomas Becket, Lady Chapel, bell tower, shrine of St David built
	Mid 14th century Remodeling with walkway to bishop's palace, wall with four gates, interior
	15th-16th century Choir and misericords, Holy Trinity Chapel, nave roof, and ceiling rebuilt
COMMISSIONED BY	King Henry I
ARCHITECTS	John Nash (1793); George Gilbert Scott (1862–70)
MATERIALS	Cambrian sandstone; Irish oak ceiling; pink marble Chapel of St Edward the Confessor
STYLE	Norman, Romanesque, Gothic, Decorated, Perpendicular (Holy Trinity Chapel)

Between the 19th and 21st centuries there has been significant restoration work including the introduction of a rose window in the 1950s and a chapel to St Edward the Confessor.

A ruined façade in the bishop's palace on the grounds.

Facing page:
St David's Cathedral stands in a dip in the ground, hiding it from view from the sea.

Additional Cathedrals

AUSTRALIA

St Peter's Cathedral, Adelaide
19th century
Gothic

Cathedral of St Stephen,
Brisbane
1862–1922
Gothic Revival

St Paul's Cathedral, Melbourne
19th century
Gothic Revival

AUSTRIA

Cathedral of the Immaculate Conception
(New Cathedral), Linz
19th–20th century
Gothic

BRAZIL

Catedral Metropolitana Nossa Senhora
Aparecida, Brasilia
1970
Modern

Cathedral of Our Lady of Lourdes,
Canela,
Rio Grande do Sul
1953–87
English Gothic

Cathedral Basilica of Salvador,
Salvador
17th century
Portuguese Mannerist

São Paulo Cathedral,
São Paulo
1913–54
New Gothic

CHINA

Cathedral of the Immaculate
Conception, Beijing
17th century, 20th century
Baroque

Cathedral of the Sacred Heart,
Guangzhou
19th century
Gothic

St Ignatius Cathedral, Shanghai
1905–10
Gothic

COLOMBIA

Catedral Primada, Bogota
1672–1792
Iberian Classicism, Baroque,

CROATIA

Cathedral of the Assumption of Virgin
Mary, Zagreb
13th century
Romanesque, Neo-Gothic

CUBA

San Cristóbal Cathedral, Havana
1748–89
Late Baroque

EGYPT

St Mark's Cathedral, Alexandria
4th century CE, 19th, 20th century
Coptic Orthodox

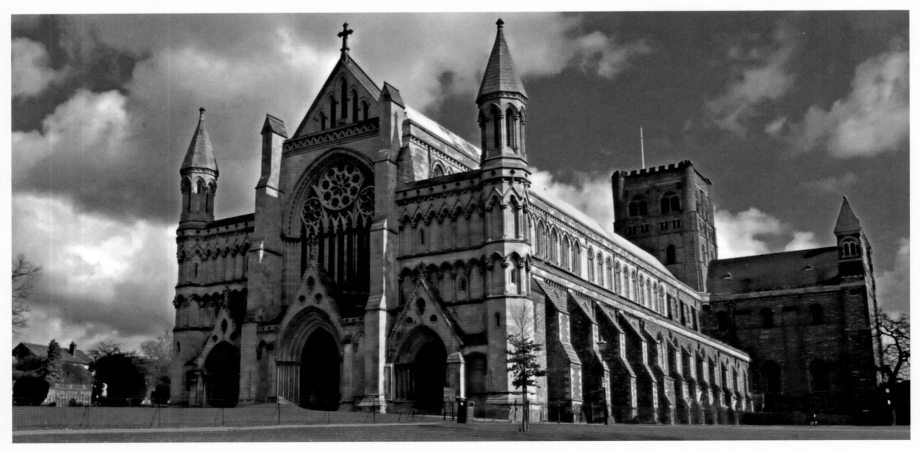

St Alban's Cathedral, St Alban, England.

ENGLAND

Cathedral Church of the Holy and Undivided Trinity, Bristol, Bristol
1140–1526
Norman, Gothic, Gothic Revival

Cathedral Church of the Holy and Undivided Trinity, Carlisle, Cumbria
1092–1527
Norman, Gothic

Cathedral Church of Christ and the Blessed Virgin Mary, Chester, Cheshire
1093–c.1530
Romanesque, Gothic

Cathedral Church of the Holy Trinity, Chichester, West Sussex
1088–1901
Norman, Gothic

Cathedral Church of Blessed Virgin Mary and St Ethelbert, Hereford, Herefordshire
1079–c. 1530
Gothic, Early English

Cathedral Church of the Blessed Virgin Mary and St Chad, Lichfield, Staffordshire
1195–c. 1385
Gothic

Cathedral Church of the Holy and Undivided Trinity, Norwich, Norfolk
1096–c.1536
Norman, Gothic

Cathedral Church of Christ, Oxford, Oxfordshire
1158–1529
Romanesque, Gothic

Cathedral Church of St Peter, St Paul, and St Andrew, Peterborough, Cambridgeshire
1117–c. 1508
Norman, Gothic

Ripon Cathedral, Ripon, North Yorkshire
1154–1522
Anglo Saxon, Gothic, Early English

Cathedral Church of Christ and the Blessed Virgin Mary, Rochester, Kent
1077–c. 1512, Norman

The Cathedral and Abbey Church of St Alban, Hertfordshire
1077–1521
Norman, Romanesque, Gothic

Cathedral and Collegiate Church of St Savior and St Mary Overie, Southwark, London
c. 1208–c. 1520
Romanesque, Gothic

Cathedral and Parish Church of the Blessed Virgin Mary, Southwell, Nottinghamshire
1108–c. 1450
Norman, Early English

Cathedral Church of Christ and the Blessed Virgin Mary, Worcester, Worcestershire
1084–1504
Norman, Gothic

Cathedral and Metropolitical Church of St Peter, York, North Yorkshire
1154–1500
Early English, Perpendicular

FRANCE

Cathedral of St Maurice, Angers
12th and 13th centuries
Gothic, Romanesque

Cathedral of St Lazare, Autun
1120–46
Romanesque

Cathédrale Notre Dame-des-Doms, Avignon
12th, 15th, 17th, 19th centuries
Romanesque

Cathedral of Our Lady of the Assumption, Clermont-Ferrand
1246–95, 1865
Gothic

Notre-Dame Cathedral, Le Puy
10th–12th centuries
Romanesque, Byzantine

St-Jean Cathedral, Lyon
1165–1480
Romanesque, Gothic

Cathédrale St-Pierre-St-Paul, Nantes
1434–end 19th century
Gothic

Notre-Dame Cathedral, Noyon
1150–1290
Romanesque, Gothic

Clermont Ferrand Cathedral, France.

St Peter's Cathedral, Poitiers
1162–1379
Gothic, Romanesque

Notre-Dame Cathedral, Rouen
1063; 1145; 1200–50
Gothic

Cathedral of St Etienne, Sens
12th–16th century
Gothic

Soissons Cathedral, Soissons
1177–13th century
Gothic

Cathedral of St Gatien, Tours
1170–1547
Romanesque, Gothic

GERMANY

Berliner Dom, Berlin
1747–50, 1894–1905
Baroque, Neo-Baroque

Munster St Martin, Bonn
1150–1230
Romanesque

Bremen Dom, Bremen
11th century
Romanesque

Hofkirche, Dresden
1738–51
Baroque

Dom St Marien, Erfurt
15th century
Gothic

Kaiserdom, Frankfurt
13th, 14th, 15th centuries
Carolingian

Freiburg Cathedral, Freiburg
13th–14th century
Gothic

St Mary's Cathedral, Hildesheim
1010–20, 1950–60
Romanesque

Cathedral of Ss Peter and Paul, Naumberg
13th, 14th, 15th, 19th centuries
Late Romanesque, Gothic

Dom St Kilian, Würzburg
1045–1188
Romanesque

GREECE

Metropolitan Cathedral of Athens,
Athens
1842–62
Greek Orthodox

HONG KONG

St John's Cathedral, Hong Kong
19th century
English and Decorated Gothic

INDIA

St Thomas Cathedral, Mumbai
1718
British Colonial

Se Cathedral of Santa Catarina, Old Goa
16th century
Portuguese Manueline

ITALY

Duomo Nuovo (New Cathedral), Brescia
1604–1825
Palladian

San Miniato al Monte, Florence
11th–13th century
Romanesque

Girona Cathedral, Girona
11th and 14th centuries
Romanesque, Gothic

Duomo di San Martino, Lucca
11th, 13th, 14th, 15th centuries
Romanesque

Cathedral-Basilica of Cefalú, Sicily
1131–1267
Norman

Verona Cathedral, Verona
12th century
Romanesque

KAZAKHSTAN

Ascension Cathedral, Almaty
1907
Russian Orthodox

LATVIA

St Mary's Cathedral, Riga
13th century; Romanesque, Baroque

LITHUANIA

St Stanislav's Cathedral, Vilnius
17th century
European Classicism

Ascension Cathedral, Almaty, Kazakhstan.

LUXEMBOURG

Notre-Dame Cathedral
Luxembourg
17th century
Gothic, Renaissance

MYANMAR

St Mary's Cathedral, Yangon
1895–99
Gothic Revival

PHILIPPINES

Iglesia de Imaculada Concepcion,
Manila
1654–71, 1863
Baroque

POLAND

Frombork Cathedral, Frombork
1342–88
Gothic

Oliwa Cathedral, Oliwa, Gdansk
Gothic
14th century
Cathedral of St John, Warsaw
15th–18th century
Gothic

Cathedral of St John the Baptist, Wroclaw
13th, 14th, 17th, 20th centuries
Baroque, Gothic

SRI LANKA

St Lucia Cathedral, Colombo
20th century
Gothic

SOUTH AFRICA

Cathedral Church of St George the Martyr,
Cape Town
1862–
Neo-Romanesque

SPAIN

Avila Cathedral, Avila
12th century
Romanesque

Barcelona Cathedral, Barcelona
1298–late 19th century
Gothic

Cadiz Cathedral, Cadiz
1722–1838; Baroque

Granada Cathedral, Granada
16th century; Gothic

Ibiza Cathedral, Ibiza
13th century
Gothic

Catedral de San Isidro, Madrid
Mid 17th century
Baroque

Almudena Cathedral, Madrid
1883-1993
Neo-Gothic, Neo-Classical

Palma Cathedral, Palma
14th–16th century
Gothic

New Cathedral, Salamanca
1513–1733
Late Gothic, Baroque

Segovia Cathedral, Segovia
1525–1678
Gothic

Iglesia de San Pedro, Teruel
17th century
Mudéjar

St Mary of Valencia Cathedral,
Valencia
13th century
Gothic

Cathedral of Zamora, Zamora
12th century
Romanesque

TURKEY

Cathedral of the Holy Spirit
19th century
Baroque

VIETNAM

Notre-Dame Cathedral,
Saigon
19th century
Gothic

USA

Cathedral of St Mary,
Miami, Florida
1955-57
Portuguese Baroque

Cathedral of the Holy Cross,
Boston, Mass.
19th century
Gothic Revival

St Mary of Valencia Cathedral, Valencia, Spain.

Glossary

Abbey A Christian monastery or convent under the governance of an abbot or abbess.

Anglicanism: Commonly refers to the beliefs and practices of a world-wide affiliation of Christian churches, most of which have historical connections with the Church of England.

Aisle: Passage running alongside the nave and separated from it by a row of columns or piers.

Ambulatory: Passage running around the apse of a church.

Apse: A semi-circular or polygonal section of the sanctuary at the liturgical east end beyond the altar.

Baldachin: A free-standing canopy supported by columns; often placed over a religious object such as a tabernacle shrine or carried in a church procession.

Baptistery: Part of a church (often detached) where baptisms are performed.

Basilica: A church with side aisles (separated from the nave by columns) and a high row of windows (the clerestory) above the aisles.

Bay: A regular division of the building defined by features such as windows, arches, columns, etc.

Blessed Sacrament: Another term for the Body and Blood of Christ. It is a devotional name used to refer to the Host and wine after they have been consecrated.

Boss(es): A projecting keystone, usually painted or carved, that forms the meeting point of the ribs of a vault.

Buttress: A vertical structure of stone or brick that supports a wall, counteracting the lateral thrust of an arch, roof, or vault.

Campanile: Italian word for bell tower, usually standing separate from the main building (usually a church).

Canon: A specific church law or decree. All canons taken together made up the body of canon law that governed the Christian church.

Capital: The molded or carved top of a column or pier that acts as the mediator between the column and the load it supports; usually decorated.

Carolingian: Of or relating to a Frankish dynasty founded by Charlemagne's father that ruled from 751 CE to 987 CE.

Chancel: Part of a church near the main altar used by the priests; open to the choir.

Chantry chapel: In English churches, a chapel for celebrating masses for the dead.

Chapel: A small place for worship; part of a large church or a separate building.

Chapter House: In English cathedrals and monasteries, a room or hall for meetings of the chapter (governing body).

Chevet: Largely in French architecture, the east end of a church formed by the apse, ambulatory, and chapels.

Choir (quire): Usually in the western part of the chancel between the nave and the sanctuary. It is occasionally located in the eastern part of the nave.

Choirscreen: The partition made of wood or stone, often decorated with carvings and paintings, that separates the space of the clergy (chancel) from that of the laity (nave). (Also see Rood-screen)

Cistercian: Cistercian architecture is associated with the churches, monasteries, and abbeys of the Roman Catholic Cistercian Order. It was simple and utilitarian; buildings were made, where possible, of smooth, pale stone.

Clerestory: The topmost story of a nave wall, pierced by windows.

Cloister: In a monastery, a quadrangular space surrounded by roofed or vaulted passages that link the church with the domestic areas; the inner walls of the passages open onto the quadrangle through colonnades.

Close: The precinct or grounds of an English cathedral.

Collegiate church: A church served and administered by a college of canons presided over by a dean or provost. Its governance is similar to that of a cathedral though it is not the seat of a bishop.

Compound pier: A pier formed by a bundle of shafts or by a solid core surrounded byu attached or detached columns.

Concordat: A *concordat* is an agreement between the Holy See and the government of a country on religious matters.

Crossing: The central space at the intersection of the nave and transepts; usually surmounted by a tower or dome.

Crypt: Also called lower church, it is a chamber or vault under a church, usually at the east end and often containing graves or relics.

Diocese: An administrative territorial unit administered by a bishop. An important diocese is called an archdiocese which is governed by an archbishop.

Dissolution of monasteries: The appropriation of the property and assets of the English and Welsh monasteries (1536–40) by Henry VIII. It was meant to weaken the power of the church and replenish the treasury.

Engaged column: A column attached to the pier or wall behind it.

Episcopate: The collective body of all bishops of a church. In such churches it is held that only a person in apostolic succession (a line of succession dating back to the Apostles) can be a bishop, the only person who can validly ordain Christian clergy .

Eucharist: Also known as Holy Communion.

Flying buttress: A type of buttress used to transmit the horizontal force of a vaulted ceiling through the walls and across an intervening space (eg. of an aisle, chapel, or cloister) to a counterweight outside the building.

Gable: The triangle formed by a sloping roof; can sometimes be arched or stepped, and may be used as a pure decorative form.

Gallery: In a church, a balcony for separating specific groups (the court, women) during a service.

Holy See: It is the episcopal jurisdiction of the Catholic Church in Rome in which its bishop is commonly known as the Pope. It forms the central government of the church.

Galero: In the Roman Catholic Church this is a large, broad-brimmed tasseled hat worn by clergy.

Greek cross: Cross with arms of equal length.

Groin vault: A vault formed by the intersection at right angles of two barrel vaults.

Hall church: Church with nave and side aisles of approximately equal height, often united under a single immense roof. Particularly common in German Gothic.

Iconostasis: In Eastern Christianity a wall of icons and religious paintings, separating the nave from the sanctuary in a church.

Indulgence: In Roman Catholic theology a full or partial indulgence was the remission of temporary punishment due to sins which have already been forgiven. It is granted by the church after the sinner has confessed and received absolution. Indulgences were a major point of contention when Martin Luther initiated the Protestant Reformation.

Inquisition: A tribunal set up by the church to suppress heresy. Formally inaugurated in 1231 by Pope Gregory to investigate heresy among the Cathars of southern France.

Lantern: (Lantern tower) A windowed turret set on a dome or roof; used to provide light ato the area below

Marian: Relating to the Blessed Virgin Mary.

Misericord: Mercy seat. A small wooden shelf on the underside of a folding seat in a church, installed to provide a degree of comfort for a person who has to stand during long periods of prayer.

Monastery: the complex of buildings used by a community of monks. Includes church, cloister, chapter house, refectory, dormitory.

Monstrance: The vessel, usually ornate, used to display the consecrated Eucharistic Host at Mass and certain ceremonies.

Narthex: The large porch or vestibule across the main (west) entrance to medieval churches.

Nave: The central approach to the High Altar extending from the entry to the chancel, flanked by aisles separated by an arcade.

Obelisk: A four-sided column tapering to a pyramid or cone.

Ogee arch: Arch formed by four curves, the two convex curves below becoming concave curves that meet in a sharp point.

Openwork: A pierced surface or wall made up of finely carved tracery.

Oratory: A small private chapel.

Pier: A large, solid, and free-standing support, usually square or round in section.

Pinnacle: A small turret-like architectural feature, often richly ornamented, that crowns parapets, pediments above windows or doors, flying buttresses, spires, etc.

Poor Man's Bible: Refers to various forms of Christian art (paintings, carvings, mosaics, and stained glass) that were primarily in churches and cathedrals to illustrate the teachings of the Bible. These art forms were very popular in the Middle Ages and intended to educate the largely illiterate population about Christianity.

Portico: Porch or walkway supported by columns, the covered entrance to a building.

Presbytery: Area of a church to the east of the choir reserved for the clergy.

Priory: A house of men or women under religious vows headed by a prior or prioress.

Radiating chapels: Chapels situated on the ambulatory of a semicircular or polygonal choir.

Reconquista: (Spa). Gradual reconquest by Christian forces of the Spanish and Portuguese kingdoms held by the Moors, who had conquered much of the Iberian peninsula in the early 8th century. It finally ended in 1492 when the Moors lost Granada.

Reformation: 16th-century movement that began as a search for reform within the Roman Catholic Church and led to the establishment of Protestantism. Leading figures were Martin Luther, Jan Hus, and John Calvin.

Reliquary: A decorated container for sacred relics, usually parts of a saint's body.

Retable: A painting or sculpted panel behind an altar.

Retrochoir: Area of choir behind the High Altar.

Ribbed vault: A vault in which the thrust is carried entirely by a framework of diagonal ribs.

Rood-screen: (Also see Choir-screen) The rood-screen was surmounted by a cross (rood) and sometimes used as a singers' gallery.

Rose window: A circular window, usually large, filled with tracery.

Royal Peculiar: A place of worship that falls directly under the jurisdiction of the British monarch, rather than a diocese.

Spanish Inquisition: Funded by Ferdinand and Isabella of Spain in 1478 it was intended to maintain Catholic orthodoxy in their kingdoms and replace the medieval inquisition which was under papal control. It played a leading role in the persecution of recent converts, particularly Jews and Moors, who had been coerced on pain of death to adopt the Christian religion.

Theotokos: A title of Mary, the mother of Jesus, used especially in the Eastern Orthodox and other eastern churches. (Literal translation: God-bearer and the one who gives birth to God).

Transubstantiation: The change of the substance of bread and wine into the Body and Blood (respectively) of Christ in the Eucharist.

Undercroft: A cellar or underground room used for storage. The term is sometimes used to describe a crypt beneath a church, used for burial purposes.

Westwerk: (Ger.) The monumental, west-facing entrance section of a Carolingian, Ottonian, or Romanesque church.

STYLES

Decorated: The second major style of Gothic architecture in England (c. 1240-1330), noted for the development of ornate tracery and the use of ogee arches. It was followed by Perpendicular.

Early English: The first major style of Gothic architecture in England (c. 1170-1240).

Flamboyant: The last major style of French Gothic architecture, so called because of its highly elaborate 'flame-like' tracery.

Gothic: Originating in 12th-century France and lasting into the 16th century, the style flourished during the high and late medieval period.
It evolved from Romanesque architecture and was succeeded by Renaissance architecture.

Gothic Revival: (or Neo-Gothic) A 19th-century revival of the Gothic style.

Manueline: A late Gothic and early Renaissaance decorative style in Portugal in the early 16th century (named after Manuel I).

Mozarabic: Spanish style of art and architecture influenced by Islamic styles.

Mujédar: (Arabic) Spanish style of decorative art based on the imitation of Islamic forms.

Perpendicular: The last of the three major styles of Gothic architecture in England (c. 1330-1530). It is characterized by comparatively simple decoration and soaring vertical lines. It was preceded by the Decorated style.

Plateresque: A highly ornate style of architectural decoration that flourished in Spain during the late 15th and early 16th centuries.

Rayonnant: Style of Gothic architecture flourishing in France from the mid 13th to mid 14th century, characterized by greater use of stained glass and by the radiating tracery of its rose windows.

Romanesque: It combined features of Western Roman and Byzantine. Characterized by semi-circular arches. Ranging from 6th to 10th centuries. In England, it was known as Norman.

Picture Credits

Front Cover: Hien It (Flickr Creative Commons)

p2 (Wikimedia Commons); p6-7 gatefold: Canalletto painting of Westminster Abbey (Wikimedia Commons), Chartres Cathedral rose window, Tony Hisgett (Flickr Creative Commons), Mezquita dome, Cordoba, Frank Kovalchek (Flickr Creative Commons), St Paul's Cathedral, Steve Cadman (Flickr Creative Commons); p8 (Wikimedia Commons); p9 *top* Urban (Wikimedia Commons), *bottom* (Wikimedia Commons); p10 Adrian Pingstone (Wikimedia Commons); p11 Rita1234 (Wikimedia Commons); p12 Phil Whitehouse (Wikimedia Commons); p13 *top* Christopher Kramer (Wikimedia Commons), *bottom* ecelan (Wikimedia Commons); p14 Benh LIEU SONG (Wikimedia Commons); p15 tympanum, Bernard Gagnon (Wikimedia Commons), rood-screen, Jastrow (Wikimedia Commons), pulpit, Alaexis (Wikimedia Commons), reredos, Chris Light (Wikipedia), retable, Jacopo Durandi (Wikimedia Commons); p16 Geoff Penaluna (Flickr Creative commons); p17 *top* (Wikipedia), *bottom* (Wikimedia Commons); p18 Swamibu (Flickr Creative Commons); p19 *top & bottom* Jason7825 (Wikimedia Commons); p20 (Wikimedia Commons); p21 *top & bottom* de:Benutzer:Griensteidl (Wikimedia Commons); p22 Leon Reed (Flickr Creative Commons); p23 *top* David Monniaux (Wikipedia), *bottom* William M Connolley (Wikipedia); p24 Brad Smith (Flickr Creative Commons); p25 *top* Aconcagua (Wikimedia Commons), *bottom* Matthias Kable (Wikimedia Commons); p26 (Wikimedia Commons); p27 *top* Jean-Pol GRANDMONT (Wikimedia Commons), *bottom* Martin Beek (Flickr Creative Commons); p28 Yabby (Flickr Creative Commons); p29 *top* Pbrundel (Wikimedia Commons), *bottom* Harmonia Amanda (Wikimedia Commons); p30 Moody 75 (Flickr Creative Commons); p31 *top & bottom* (Wikimedia Commons); p32 Maribelle71 (Flickr Creative Commons); p33 *top & bottom* Piotr Kuczyński (Wikimedia Commons); p34 Klearchos Kapoutsis (Flickr Creative Commons); p35 *top* (Wikimedia Commons), *bottom* Elena Chochkova (Wikimedia Commons); p36 (Wikimedia Commons); p37 *top* Poco a poco (Wikimedia Commons), *bottom* Laura Padgett (Flickr Creative Commons); p38 Johnny Lang (Flickr Creative Commons); p39 *top & bottom* Tango7174 (Wikimedia Commons); p40 Harold Slatore (Flickr Creative Commons); p41 *top* Brandon Godfrey (Wikimedia Commons), *bottom* marbla123 (Flickr Creative Commons); p42 Br Lawrence Lew, O.P. (Flickr Creative Commons); p43 *top & bottom* László Szalai (Beyond silence) (Wikimedia Commons); p44 o¬ (Flickr Creative Commons); p45 *top* Martin Kozák (Wikimedia Commons), *bottom* Pudelek (Marcin Szala) (Wikimedia Commons); p46 Corbis (CSM107329); p47 *top* FaceMePLS (Flickr Creative Commons), *bottom* smaedli (Flickr Creative Commons); p48 Joe Dunckley (Flickr Creative Commons); p49 *top* Bernard Gagnon (Wikimedia Commons), *bottom* (Wikipedia); p50 Simon Phipps (Flickr Creative Commons); p51 *top* Syuu (Flickr Creative Commons), *bottom* Hyougushi (Flickr Creative Commons); p52 Neil Howard (Flickr Creative Commons); p53 *top* Markhillary (Flickr Creative Commons), *bottom* Mattana (Wikimedia Commons); p54 (Wikimedia Commons); p55 *top* Hans A Rosbach (Wikimedia Commons), *bottom* Brighton (Flick Creative Commons); p56 Paul Watson (Flickr Creative Commons); p57 *top* Carcharoth (commons) (Wikimedia Commons), *bottom* Immanuel Giel (Wikimedia Commons); p58 Sarunas Mikalauskas (Flickr Creative Commons); p59 *top* Nigel's Europe (Flickr Creative Commons), *bottom* (Wikipedia); p60 (Wikimedia Commons); p61 *top & bottom* (Wikipedia); p62 Stephen Jones (Flickr Creative Commons); p63 *top* Matt Gibson (Wikimedia Commons), *bottom* (Flickr Creative Commons); p64 (Wikimedia Commons); p65 *top* Bernard Gagnon (Wikimedia Commons), *bottom* Kjetil Bjørnsrud (Wikipedia); p66 Adrian Midgley (Flickr Creative Commons); p67 *top* Wanner-Laufer (Wikimedia Commons), *bottom* Ellan Vannin (Flickr Creative Commons); p68 Lauren (Flickr Creative Commons); p69 *top* Mendhak (Flickr Creative Commons), *bottom* Morgaine (Flickr Creative Commons); p70 Chilli Head (Flickr Creative Commons); p71 *top* Robin Iversen Rönnlund (Flickr Creative Commons), *bottom* Benjamin Haines (Flickr Creative Commons); p72 Christine (Flickr Creative Commons); p73 *top* Pertsabov (Wikipedia), *bottom* the girl (Flickr Creative Commons); p74 Christina T (Flickr Creative Commons); p75 *top* Jonathan M (Wikipedia), *bottom* Coyau (Wikipedia); p76 Andy Hawkins (Flickr Creative Commons); p77 *top* Jean Marie Desbois Wikipedia), *bottom* (Wikipedia); p78 Eisenstein (Flickr Creative Commons); p79 *top* (Wikipedia), *bottom* Tango7174 (Wikipedia); p80 Jean-Pierre Dalbéra (Flickr Creative Commons); p81 *top* (Wikimedia Commons), *bottom* Vassil (Wikimedia Commons); p82 Steve Cadman (Flickr Creative Commons); p83 (Wikimedia Commons), *bottom* (Wikipedia); p84 Andrew Sweeney (Flickr Creative Commons); p85 *top* KoS (Wikimedia Commons), *bottom* AEngineer (Flickr Creative Commons); p86 Daxis (Flickr Creative Commons); p87 *top* AEngineer (Flickr Creative Commons), *bottom* (Wikipedia); p88 (Wikimedia Commons); p89 *top* Benh LIEU SONG (Wikimedia Commons), *bottom* Fortune carrée (Flickr Creative Commons); p90 (Wikimedia Commons); p91 *top* Joel Mann (Flickr Creative Commons), *bottom* Jaydubyasee (Flickr Creative Commons); p92 Holly Hayes (Flickr Creative Commons); p93 *top* AlphaTangoBravo / Adam Baker (Flickr Creative Commons), *bottom* Pom2 (Wikimedia Commons); p94 Hühnerauge (Flickr Creative Commons); p95 *top & bottom* Lokilech (Wikipedia); p96 Ian Griffiths (Flickr Creative Commons); p97 *top & bottom* (Wikimedia Commons); p98 Luhai Wong (Flickr Creative Commons); p99 *top* Sven Petersen (Wikimedia Commons), *bottom* de:Benutzer:Moguntiner (Wikipedia); p100 (Wikimedia Commons); p101 *top* dsa66503 (Flickr Creative Commons), *bottom* (Wikimedia Commons); p102 Robert Scarth (Flickr Creative Commons); p103 *top* (Wikimedia Commons), *bottom* Matthias Rosenkranz (Flickr Creative Commons); p104 Andre M Hünseler (Flickr Creative Commons); p105 *top* T Voekler (Wikimedia

Facing page: Frombork Cathedral, Frombork, Poland.